THE SECRETS
OF THE
BULLETPROOF
SPIRIT

BALLANTINE BOOKS   NEW YORK

THE SECRETS OF THE BULLETPROOF SPIRIT

. . .

*How to Bounce Back
from Life's Hardest Hits*

Azim Khamisa and *Jillian Quinn*

Published in the United States by Ballantine Books, an imprint of
The Random House Publishing Group, a division of
Random House, Inc., New York.

BALLANTINE and colophon are registered trademarks of Random House, Inc.

Library of Congress Cataloging-in-Publication Data
Khamisa, Azim.
The secrets of the bulletproof spirit : how to bounce back from
life's hardest hits / Azim Khamisa and Jillian Quinn.
p. cm.
ISBN 978-0-345-50603-0 (hardcover : alk. paper)
1. Resilience (Personality trait) I. Quinn, Jillian. II. Title.
BF698.35.R47K43 2009
155.2'4—dc22   2008045269

Printed in the United States of America on acid-free paper

www.ballantinebooks.com

2 4 6 8 9 7 5 3 1

First Edition

Book design by Susan Turner

ACKNOWLEDGMENTS

Azim

My deepest thanks to the following: My family, for their ever-lasting and ever-loving support of my work; the Donors, Staff, Board, and volunteers of TKF, for their passion, generosity, and commitment to serve children and youth; the staff and many caregivers of the CANEI program and NYAP's leadership and staff, for their commitment to CANEI and the youth it serves; Ples Felix and Tony Hicks, who are important and integral parts of my story and work; my team at ANK, for supporting my busy speaking schedule; and finally, and most important, Jillian Quinn, for her compassion, energy, and creativity. She has my utmost gratitude and respect.

Jillian

Though writing is an intensely solitary endeavor, bringing a book into the world takes a village. To the wonderful souls in my village, I am forever grateful:

First of all, Azim Khamisa, for embodying the essence of the bulletproof spirit and for taking this journey with me; from both authors to Bill Gladstone, whose counsel and practical expertise made the road smooth; Marnie Cochran, for being the kind of editor most writers only get to dream about working with; Christina Duffy for her help with all the details; also, many thanks to Libby McGuire, Kim Hovey, Katie O'Callaghan, Christine

Cabello, Stacey Witcraft, Brian McLendon, Diana Franco, Lisa Barnes, Beck Stvan, Eric Fuentecilla, Lea Beresford, and Shona McCarthy, for their vision, genius, and generous support; Gina Centrello and Mary Belmonte, who appear to be people but are really angels—there are no words to adequately convey the depths of my gratitude; Frank Madden, David Kin, Peter Martin, Tim Bassett, and Katie Davidson, for their invaluable contributions to my life; the Quinn clan, for surrounding me with strength and simple goodness; Jenny Markert, Cheryl Herman, Devoney Looser, Mary Mellett, Margaret MacDonald, Susan de Haan, Rebecca Correllus, Jeannie Chory, Katie Odell, Carol Acquilano, Claire Klenosky, Kim Marchese, Alicia Jazayeri, and Kirsten Rappleyea, for love and sisterhood; Karen Sparks, for things only another writer could understand; Cindy Guardiola, who put her mind, heart, soul, and countless hours into this book and who made me laugh and caught my tears, too; my sisters, Susan Meyer and Kate Howlett, for all we've shared and always will; my father, for teaching me to swim in every sense of the word; my mother—on every level imaginable, I could not have written this book without you; my beautiful children, Teddy, Mia, and Katie Wen, for filling my life with sweetness and my heart with more love than I knew existed; and, finally, to Chris, for finding me and keeping me and for walking this world by my side.

CONTENTS

AUTHORS' NOTE

Throughout the book, you will notice that we use one voice. Though we made a practical decision to use one voice (Jillian's) to make communication with you less awkward and more intimate, please know that every idea and aspect of this book comes from the minds and hearts of both authors.

INTRODUCTION

THINK BACK TO WHEN YOU WERE A KID. MAYBE YOU GREW UP watching Superman, Batman, and Wonder Woman on Saturday mornings like we did. Maybe you liked your favorite superhero so much you turned your bedsheet into a cape and pretended to *be* him or her! Supercool outfits and gadgets aside, what made superheroes so attractive to us was their invincibility. They could run into burning buildings and come out unscathed and be hit by bullets and remain unharmed. They could take any hit and come out on top. Our favorite superheroes always bounced back!

But that was then and this is now. You're all grown up, you live in the *real* world, and the cape doesn't cut it anymore. No costume you put on can protect you from the bad stuff out there. The "bullets" that come your way are physical, emotional, and financial. Maybe you took a heartbreaking hit early on in the form of a dysfunctional family life or challenging childhood. Maybe you can't help noticing that all around you people are being hit with depression and illness, by relationship blowups and meltdowns, and in their wallets and pension funds. Maybe you've started tallying the losses you see your family and friends taking—their hair, their figures, their breasts, their spouses, their jobs, their investments, their youth, and their peace of mind. Maybe you've taken (or live in fear of taking) a hit that's truly heartbreaking—the death of a loved one, the diagnosis of a frightening disease, or the betrayal of a sacred trust. Or maybe you just want to prepare yourself for the inevitable. With so many bullets flying, it's enough to make you wish you *were* made of steel.

Every human being is vulnerable to the physical, emotional, and financial hits that life hands out, but there *are* people walking through the world *spiritually bulletproof.* People with super spiritual resiliency take as many hard hits as anyone else, but they always bounce back and wind up on top. They lose jobs, relationships, health, and money just like the rest of us, but they don't stay defeated. When compared with their spiritually fragile counterparts, spiritually bulletproof people derive many benefits from their resiliency, including:

- more career satisfaction
- deeper and more intimate relationships
- better health
- greater financial success
- higher levels of confidence

In fact, spiritual resiliency—more than education, intelligence, and wealth—is one of the strongest predictors of happiness.

If you're looking to be happier, your spiritual resiliency is worth working on because it impacts literally every other area of your life and has the power to magnify the good and mitigate the bad in all you experience. And in terms of spiritual resiliency, this may be the most important book you will ever read. We know that's a pretty big claim, but this book gives you the inside track to taking *any* hit and coming out on top. It shows you *exactly* what to do to increase your spiritual resiliency by helping you to understand the way that spiritually bulletproof people *think.*

In the thirty short chapters of this book, you will learn why some people are able to take life's heartbreaking hits and come out on top, while others are completely derailed by obstacles, heartbreak, and adversity. You will understand the way that certain thoughts and behaviors contribute to spiritual fragility and why many people choose to play the victim their whole lives rather than find the spiritual hero within. You will make connections between the kind of thinking and behavior you may have grown up seeing and the way you view things now. With an understanding of those patterns, you will begin to think more spiritually affirming thoughts and make more spiritually empowering choices. And you will learn to "anchor" your new knowledge by using integration techniques that really work. While there's no way to stop the bullets that are flying and there's no foolproof plan for staying out of the line of fire, the information, inspiration, and tools you'll find in this book will provide you with a kind of "bulletproof vest." You may get floored, have the wind knocked out of you, and even have some nasty bruises, but you *will* be able to stand up again and face another day. What's more, you'll learn how the hit you've taken can fuel your personal evolution and actually help you to create the life of your dreams. When you connect with your bulletproof spirit, there's nothing that can keep you down for the count. Are you ready to bounce back?

DOCTORS WILL SOMETIMES ASK PATIENTS TO DESCRIBE PHYSICAL pain on a scale from one to ten, with one being very mild and ten being agony. Well, hits fall along the heartbreak scale in much the same way. Most of the hits we take are somewhere in the middle of the scale—high enough to be noticed but not the worst we can imagine—though how we score them is totally subjective. Most of us take many minor and moderate hits that end up taking a cumulative toll over the long haul. If, like me, you start out with a growing-up experience that was "challenging," you may take your first serious hit before you even know that life offers any alternatives. And then the hits just keep on coming. Like the hit I took at age twenty-four when a reckless driver left me with a permanent neurological injury that enrolled me in the school of serious chronic pain and still affects me on a daily basis more than fifteen years later. It's hard to put a number on that hit because it is a hit I must take anew each day. I know enough about the world now to realize, in the big scheme of things, this hit is really probably a five or six, but there are some days when it can still feel like an eight or nine. And then there are the hits that break your heart into a million little pieces in one sickening second but from which you recover so fully that what you once thought a ten becomes half that through the power of perspective, time, and healing. When I was in my early thirties, I was almost six months pregnant with my third child and thrilled to be expanding my family. I traded in my car for a minivan, started decorating the nursery, and even made arrangements to take time off from a teaching position at a local college. I had made it through the first few miserable months of morning-noon-and-night-sickness, and was in that magical sixth month of pregnancy—my skin was glowing, my hair was shiny, and I was filling out maternity clothes with a cute baby bump.

One gorgeous April morning, I strapped my four-year-old son and one-year-old daughter into their car seats and drove to my midwife's office for a routine prenatal visit. Teddy, my little boy, was old enough to be excited to hear his baby sister's heartbeat and to go out to Friendly's for lunch afterward. I remember rolling the windows down and singing in the car with my kids—it was a really beautiful morning and I felt so blessed and so filled with life.

At the office, when the midwife couldn't find the baby's heartbeat, I tried to push down my panic and believe the midwife's reassurances that the baby was probably just facing away from the stethoscope. I tried to keep calm while they ushered me to the hospital's sonogram suite to see what was going on. As I lay with the cold sonogram jelly dripping down my very pregnant belly, I kept one hand on my toddler and another on my heart, which felt as if it was going to jump right out of my chest.

When the technician wouldn't tell me anything, I tried to believe that the look I saw in her eyes was something other than what I knew it was. But then the midwife came back in and said "Jillian, I'm so sorry. The baby's heart has stopped and we're not sure why. I'm terribly sorry, but she's gone." I sat up and lifted my two little children onto the table and had to tell them that their baby sister had gone to heaven. I held them and tried to explain things in a way they would understand and, on the surface, I kept it together. But inside, I felt as if I might collapse and die. I was so far along in the pregnancy that I was going to have to be induced and go through labor and delivery of my dead baby or have a major surgery and deal with that aftermath. When I finally got home, I had my husband take the kids out of the house and, in the privacy of my bedroom, cried so hard that I broke blood vessels in my eyes. My whole body ached with grief and anger and loss. But even that first day I knew somewhere deep inside that not only would I survive this heartbreaking hit, I would somehow find and make meaning from it. I knew I could come out on top. My perspective was limited by my own heart-wrenching grief, but I was able to whisper a faint "We shall see."

You see, I had already spent years of my life connecting with my own bulletproof spirit using and living the secrets shared in this book. And so when this terrible blow came along, I was able to rely on my well-developed spiritual resiliency. At the moment, I could see no larger plan and I could never have imagined what my future held, but I did know that more would be revealed and that I could get through this and find my way to a brighter day.

Three years later, my husband and I traveled to Southern China to adopt a fourteen-month-old baby girl from an orphanage filled with beautiful baby girls whose birth mothers lived in a world of cruel circumstances and unimaginable pressures. When I met my daughter, she had never had a bath, was in need of medical attention, and slept with no mattress in a metal crib in a sweltering room with dozens of other babies. My daughter is now four and she is my pearl of great price, ransomed from a sea of loss and an ocean of red tape. She is my daughter and I am her mother *only* because in my past, I lost a daughter and, in her past, she lost a mother. I look into her beautiful little eyes and see the manifestation of both of our bulletproof spirits and I sink to my knees in gratitude for all of the moments of my life, even the heartbreaking ones. I wrote this book to collect in one concise place the secrets it took me decades of my life to learn. I wrote this book for myself, for my children, and for you, my fellow marchers in the great hit parade of life.

WHILE MY EXPERIENCE HAS BEEN WITH THE CUMULATIVE EFFECT OF the many hits life hands out, Azim's experience has been more about the way that one tragic and epic hit can change life entirely and forever. He can't give his hit a "number," because some hits are of such magnitude that no scale can measure them, no number can contain them.

When Azim was in his mid-forties, he was living a charmed life as a highly successful international investment banker, and his days were filled with friends, family, and travel. He enjoyed spending time with his twenty-year-old son, Tariq, who was an art student at nearby San Diego State University. He had taken many hits in his life, but none could have prepared him for what he was about to face. On January 22, 1995, he woke up to find that his entire life had been destroyed in one senseless moment. He had just returned from a profitable business trip the night before and had gone to sleep a happy man. When his housekeeper arrived in the morning, she handed him a business card that she had found tucked inside the screen door. The card belonged to a homicide detective with the San Diego police, and on the back was a handwritten note asking Azim to call. When he dialed the number, he received the news that his only son had been shot and killed by a member of a street gang. While Azim had been sleeping soundly the night before, he had no way of knowing that twelve miles away, his boy lay dead, his feet sticking grotesquely out of the faded Volkswagen in which he'd been shot. He had been delivering pizzas as a part-time job to earn spending money, an innocent in the wrong place at the wrong time.

Azim says that when he learned that his boy was dead, it was as if a nuclear bomb detonated inside of his heart. The pain he felt was so extreme that he felt himself leave his body. If you ask him, he will tell you that he went into the loving arms of God, where he was held for the longest time. And when he returned to his body, though he was still drowning in grief and loss, he came back with a stunning phrase formed in his mind: *There were victims on both ends of that gun.*

In the days that followed, Azim was in a haze of grief and pain. He had to tell Tariq's mother, sister, and grandparents the news he knew would shatter them. When his best friend, a normally spiritual and gentle person, expressed the desire for vengeance against his son's killer, Azim was filled again with the understanding that *there were victims on both ends of the gun.* He had no idea at that moment how important this insight would be to the rest of his life.

When his son was buried, more than 1,400 people attended the service to pay their final respects. Following the ritual tradition of his faith, Azim entered the grave to accept his son's shrouded body. It had been raining, and as he stood holding his son for the last time in a muddy grave, Azim wanted to stay in the grave with him.

In the days, weeks, and months that followed, he couldn't eat or sleep. He could barely get out of bed. Thoughts of suicide flashed through his mind and he found it impossible to imagine himself ever smiling or laughing again. In Azim's faith and tradition, grieving is observed for forty days. Grieving past this time is thought to impede the soul's journey. A spiritual teacher gave Azim this advice: "Life on earth is much more difficult than in the spiritual realm. The departed soul is quite happy on the other side. Your son has completed his assignment here. You are not grieving for his discomfort. You are feeling sorry for yourself.

Instead, do something good in his name. It will be good for you. It will be good for the recipient. It will be good for Tariq's soul." The wisdom of this philosophy rang true to him, and in it he glimpsed a path that would take him out of his grief-stricken, paralyzed state. He began to consider how this tragedy could be made into something meaningful and beautiful.

The rest of this story is nothing short of miraculous. Azim reached out to his son's killer and to his family. He forgave the young man for the murder and became close friends with his guardian and grandfather. Azim has spent the past decade working to end youth violence and to prevent the kind of tragedy both of their families have had to endure. He has devoted his life to this cause, and through his work with the Tariq Khamisa Foundation, he has touched the lives of millions of people, traveling all over the country, inspiring people with his message of forgiveness. He wrote this book because his ability to endure and transcend this heartbreaking hit was rooted in a solid foundation of spiritual resiliency. Though he learned many incredible lessons through this loss, he already knew many of the secrets this book shares, and if they helped him come out on top, be assured that they will help you, too. Though a bullet literally ripped Azim's life apart, he is living proof that the spirit really *is* bulletproof. He wrote this book so that you can benefit from the concepts and strategies that saved his life and have inspired millions of people around the world. Without these strategies, we would not be living the joyful lives we are living today—in fact, we might not be here at all.

SOMETIMES A PICTURE REALLY *IS* WORTH A THOUSAND WORDS, AND this book will give you thirty snapshots of the ways that spiritually bulletproof people think. Some of the ideas we'll share will be familiar to you, but many may challenge your current views. Some concepts or strategies may even feel threatening or annoying to you. You might find yourself thinking that some things we suggest are too idealistic or that they won't work in *your* situation. We ask you to be willing to let go of your preconceived ideas about dealing with adversity and remain receptive to receiving guidance that may challenge the way you've always thought or done things. Carl Jung believed that "There is no birth of consciousness without pain," and this book *will* take you to the next level of spiritual resiliency, but you must be willing to endure a little discomfort as you let go of what's not working in your mind and in your life. These strategies have worked for countless people we've taught and coached. Give yourself a chance to integrate them, and we know they can work for you, too.

By the way, the exercises in the Bounce Back Boot Camp sections at the end of each chapter only work if you actually *do* them! These activities help you make the leap from bulletproof *thinking* to bulletproof *living*. The newest research into how people learn shows that people change and grow most dramatically and efficiently when they actually *do* something—no matter how small—with the information or concepts they're trying to integrate. The processes and rituals embedded in these exercises are deceptively simple, but don't let their lightness fool you—they are powerfully healing and transformative. At the very minimum, choose *one* from each section and give yourself the gift of taking time out to do it. If you do them *all,* you will change your life dramatically. You will need a journal for some of them, so find a little notebook that you enjoy writing in and dedicate it to your own bulletproof spirit.

In the end, each of our lives is a series of stories—some beautiful, some heartbreaking, some terrifying, some joyful. Our lives and all their moments—the best *and* the worst—really do matter in the grand scheme of things. Every person who reads this book is connected to us and to you—we are all in this together.

As the thirty secrets unfold for you in the pages of this book, we would be honored if you would think of us as your partners in this journey of transformation and healing. When you find yourself feeling sad, overwhelmed, angry, or just plain "stuck" because of the hit you've taken, remember that you've got your very own bounce-back buddies, crisis coaches, and adversity advisors waiting to connect with you here in the pages of this book or just a few clicks away at our website, **www.bulletproof spirit.com**. Remember that deep down, on the level of our bulletproof spirits, there is no separation between us. Time and space are just illusions that make us feel separate. We believe in you even if you don't believe in yourself and we know that you can bounce back from whatever hits you've taken.

Part One

. . .

YOUR
BULLETPROOF
BIRTHRIGHT

Being Bulletproof Is Your Birthright

*In the midst of winter, I finally learned that
there was in me an invincible summer.*

—ALBERT CAMUS

BIRTHRIGHT IS A POWERFUL WORD. IT REFERS TO SOMETHING THAT
you are entitled to just because you *exist*. You arrived on this
planet with certain privileges and rights that cannot be taken
from you. One of the most important and sacred of these gifts is
your innate spiritual resiliency. You were born and you remain
spiritually bulletproof, but you may not know about this birthright
or how to go about claiming it. You already *are* the bulletproof
spirit we refer to in this book, but until you claim this part of
your identity, you won't be able to take advantage of the amazing benefits that are due you. This book is your personal guide
to claiming what is rightfully yours.

The foundation of super spiritual resiliency is extremely simple. Spiritually bulletproof people identify most strongly with their
spirits—more than with their bodies, their emotions, their profes-

sions, their possessions, their relationships, or their finances. Though they are not naïve to the realities of this volatile and challenging world, spiritually bulletproof people believe that being *spiritually* invincible is their birthright. They consciously claim that right by identifying themselves first and most deeply with their *spirits*.

> Spiritually bulletproof people believe that being *spiritually* invincible is their birthright. They consciously claim that right by identifying themselves first and most deeply with their *spirits*.

It's really important for you to know that spiritually bulletproof people are absolutely *not* spiritually *special* people! They are no better or more "advanced" than anyone else! What they *do* have going for them is that they *know* their true spiritually resilient nature and consciously, confidently, and consistently identify themselves with their spirits more than with their material identities.

The chapters that follow will give you the inside scoop on becoming bulletproof by revealing to you *exactly* how spiritually resilient people think. But make no mistake about it—all of their thoughts stem from a solid awareness of their spiritual core. Ralph Waldo Emerson captures the essence of your bulletproof birthright in his belief that "What lies behind us and what lies before us are tiny matters compared to what lies within us." To be more spiritually resilient, you don't need to *become* anything at all. All you need to do is to uncover and get in touch with your true self. What lies within you really is more powerful than any hit you may take physically, emotionally, or materially.

Inspirational speaker and author Anthony Robbins says that "The resources we need to turn our dreams into reality are within us, merely waiting for the day when we decide to wake up and claim our birthright." Claiming your birthright as a bulletproof spirit may be the most profound decision you ever make because it will impact every single area of your life and it will also ripple out into the world around you in ways you cannot yet even imagine. All you need to get started is a firm intention and a willingness to learn some new ways of thinking and doing things.

Will the Real You Please Stand Up?

There's a story found in many cultures that Henry David Thoreau recounts in his own way in *Walden*. He writes about a king's son who is forced out of his home as a baby, and is raised by a humble woodsman far away from his birthplace. The baby grows into a boy and then into a man, the whole while believing himself to be a poor and simple member of a poor and simple tribe of people. One day, a royal minister is sent to him and he learns of his true identity. He finds out that he is not at all who he thought himself to be and that, in truth, he is a prince. This story, which appears in many times and places in different forms, speaks an important truth: We may fail to see through our material bodies and circumstances to our real nature until something or someone reveals it to us. And what we find below the surface is a spiritual core vast beyond comprehension. When you believe that you are just a collection of material identities, you are like the woodcutter's son before he understands who he really is. When you claim your birthright as a bulletproof spirit, you are like the prince who finally understands the truth.

Spiritually fragile people do not identify strongly with their spirits and, therefore, they do not have high levels of spiritual resiliency. Most people do not spend any real time or energy trying to understand who they really *are*. They unconsciously accept the view of themselves that the culture reflects back to them and believe that what they see with their eyes is the sum of all they are. More than ever, people identify themselves with what they *do* and with what they *have* rather than with who they *are*. This is an identity crisis of the worst kind because it puts all the control over personal happiness *outside* the self, where external variables can wreak havoc. We've all heard stories about people ending their lives when they lost their investments during the Wall Street crash of 1929. When they lost their fortunes, they believed they had lost everything. Though this is an extreme example of the human tendency to externalize our identities, it manifests itself in subtler ways for most people.

How Do You Identify Your Identity?

It is only natural and healthy to want career success, loving relationships, a comfortable lifestyle, financial security, and physical health and attractiveness. It's essential to properly value these things and to put energy into attaining them—*we* certainly do! What's critical to remember, though, is that (1) all of these things are vulnerable to the hits that life hands out and that (2) there is a part of yourself that lies beneath and beyond these external things that is utterly immune to the slings and arrows of life. Learning to identify most strongly with that invincible part of yourself—your spirit—is the truest security available to you. When you identify more with the external aspects of your life than with your internal, spiritual nature, you are much more vulnerable to life's heartbreaking hits and much less likely to come out on top. Here are some ways that this kind of identity crisis shows up in the real world:

- Your sense of who you are is completely dependent upon a particular job or career rather than being recognized as one *part* of your identity. While it's normal—especially in these uncertain times—to feel concern about making a living, your *entire* self-worth is wrapped up in your professional identity.
- You feel that without a certain relationship, you would be nothing. Although it is natural to feel extremely attached to a spouse, romantic partner, or other important people in your life, your entire identity is defined by a particular relationship. Your sense of self-worth hinges on someone else loving you or approving of you.
- You may derive your sense of worth from your possessions.

You find yourself comparing your "stuff" to what other people have and feel either good or bad about yourself based on how you stack up. Your self-esteem is affected by how impressive your house is to other people or even by how clean and organized your home is. You fear that people will think less of you if you don't present a well-oiled, perfect front with your clothing, car, or home.

- You may find that you can't feel good about yourself unless you look good. Maybe you don't feel lovable when you're not as thin as you think you should be. Your sense of self-worth is tied up with being attractive to other people or meeting some cultural standard for beauty that is difficult to attain. You are afraid of getting older and losing your looks, because without them, you feel worthless.
- Your finances are the sole basis by which you judge your success. You cannot feel good about yourself unless you're earning a certain amount of money. You are afraid of losing your money and feel insecure whenever you think about your finances.

If your sense of yourself is dependent on external variables such as these, of course you are afraid to take a serious hit in any of these areas. Many people believe that they will be *ruined* if they lose things like their jobs, their spouses, or their money. Spiritually bulletproof people can lose any of these things and not be destroyed. While, of course, they don't *want* to take hits in any of these areas and they do what's necessary to protect themselves, spiritually resilient people know that hits are part of life and they expect to take them. What saves the day for them when a hit actually happens is that they identify most strongly with their *spirits*. They know that no matter what happens on the outside, they truly *are* spiritually bulletproof.

Of course, it's one thing to say all of this and another to actually believe it and live that way. The twenty-nine chapters that follow will help you think like the bulletproof spirit you are, but first you must decide to claim your birthright. You can have all the benefits that come with super spiritual resiliency, but you must be willing to reconnect and identify with your spirit. The simplest way to claim this birthright is to examine and remove the barriers that stand between you and your essential bulletproof nature. This book will walk you step-by-step through this process, but only you can decide to claim what belongs to you.

When you were little, you probably believed that you were destined for great things. You thought you could do anything. Before all the conditioning you received living in a world of fearful adults, you knew yourself to be spiritually bulletproof. But then you forgot the truth about who you really are and stopped believing in your invincibility. It's as if you shut the door to a magic place inside of yourself and have spent all the intervening years forgetting it's there. Though your life may take you far and wide into the world, the most important place you'll ever visit requires that you go inward rather than outward. When you decide to reclaim your bulletproof birthright, you're beginning a journey to the greatest place on earth—and guess what? It's been inside you all along, patiently waiting for you to remember it.

* * *

Bounce Back Boot Camp

These strategies will help you claim your bulletproof birthright:

- Using your journal, draw and label the different parts of your identity. Think of yourself as a kind of onion with many layers. Your drawing may have more layers than the

healthy, attractive woman

lawyer, partner in firm

home owner, investor

wife, mother

bulletproof spirit

one in this example. Write a number value from 1 to 10 on each layer to represent how important each of these parts is to your identity. Which layer best represents how you define yourself? At this point, how important is your spirit to how you define yourself? Be really honest with yourself and see what you discover.

- Using your journal, write a letter to your spirit. Depending on your relationship with your spirit, it might start "To My Spirit: I'm not sure you're even in there anywhere . . ." or it might begin "Dear Spirit, I felt your presence all day today . . ." Whatever your current relationship with your own spirit, don't judge yourself or worry. It's normal to be so busy and overwhelmed with life and its challenges that you're really out of touch with your spirit. This book is about reconnecting and remembering, so drop your spirit a line and say hello. You are addressing a part of yourself that is real and waiting to assist you in all you do.

- Sit quietly and visualize yourself taking serious hits in each "layer of your onion." Imagine losing your ability to walk, your license to practice medicine, your spouse, whatever you're most afraid of. Pay attention to which hits are most upsetting to you. Notice how your breathing and body feel during this exercise. Acknowledge that you are vulnerable in every one of these "layers" and commit to reclaiming that part of yourself that *is* invincible—your bulletproof spirit. Finish by taking a moment to be grateful for and bless each of the "layers" that enrich your life.

- Put a 3×5 notecard on your bathroom mirror with the following affirmation written on it: "Beneath and beyond all my layers, I am a bulletproof spirit." Read it every morning and every night before bed. If you visit our website, you'll find this and other affirmations from the book that you can print and use.

• • •

Build a Bulletproof Mind

"Be master of mind rather than mastered by mind."

—Zen proverb

IF YOU WANT TO TAP INTO YOUR BULLETPROOF SPIRIT, IT IS ESSEN-tial that you begin to do something that may feel really weird at first—you must start to *think about how you think.* The fancy word for this simple but profound practice is *meta-cognition,* but you don't need to use the word to benefit from the concept. A core difference between spiritually bulletproof people and their spiritually fragile counterparts is that resilient people take time to *think* about the way their minds work and then consciously *work* with their own minds to optimize them. They know that in order to take life's losses and come out on top, they will need to use every tool at their disposal and they rightly recognize that the mind is one of the most powerful tools available to them. Notice that we call the mind a "tool." You are *not* your mind—it is simply a tool for you to use in the service of love and healing. People with low spiritual resiliency tend to accept their own mental habits without question and let their brains boss them around. If you're like most people, you've never really thought about your own mental habits— most of us are way too busy day to day to stop and consider something we take for granted. The good news is that you can easily learn how to bring your brain on board to assist you in gaining super spiritual resiliency.

> Spiritually bulletproof people learn and practice mental habits that support super spiritual resiliency.

Do you remember the United Negro College Fund's public service campaign slogan "A Mind Is a Terrible Thing to Waste"? For more than thirty years, this phrase has promoted the value of higher education for all people. But a mind can be wasted in many ways, some having nothing at all to do with formal education. If you want to be able to take any hit and come out on top, you must learn not to squander yourself with thinking that undermines your resiliency. Since our minds are one of the most powerful tools we have as we face life's challenges, spiritually bulletproof people learn and practice mental habits that support super spiritual resiliency.

Your mind is the consciousness that is experienced by your brain as thought, perception, emotion, will, memory, and imagination. How often do you stop and think *about* those thoughts, perceptions, and emotions? How often do you take the time to analyze your desires, the effect that your memories have upon you, or the role that imagination plays in your life? If you're like most people, you're so busy getting through the day that your mind is on autopilot much of the time. The problem with autopilot is that most of our thoughts while in this mode are the result of external programming that we're not even aware of and that really doesn't serve us well at all.

The Keys to the Kingdom

Mahatma Gandhi believed "A man is but the product of his thoughts. What he thinks, he becomes." The idea that your thoughts help create your reality is very comforting. It means that you have some control over your life, no matter what adversity comes your way. Though you may not have total control over what happens to you in the material world, you *can* exert control over your inner world. Think of your mind as a kind of kingdom. This kingdom needs a ruler and, obviously, that ruler should be you. Begin to think of yourself as a king or queen who rules over the kingdom of your mind. To be a good ruler, you need to know what is going on in your kingdom and you have to exert benign influence over your territory, wisely guiding your kingdom toward happiness and wellness. Especially in times of crisis, think about how important it is for a ruler to lead and influence; without such direction, a kingdom in crisis can go to hell in a handbasket pretty quickly. Just as a kingdom with an ineffective ruler finds it difficult to surmount problems and crises, a person with ineffective mental habits finds it hard to take a hit and come out on top.

In order to claim your birthright as a bulletproof spirit and start reaping the rewards of super spiritual resiliency, you need to make a commitment to building a bulletproof mind. The first order of business as you begin your mind makeover is to make sure that you have the keys to your own kingdom. That is, you need to get rid of influences over your kingdom that don't serve its highest good. Most of us go through life never really understanding how much our minds are influenced by external forces rather than internal choices. It is as though we are trying to run a kingdom using rules, customs, policies, and attitudes that we didn't choose or create and that do not serve our highest good.

Defying Gravity

The Tony Award–winning musical *Wicked* is based on a retelling of *The Wizard of Oz* from the point of view of Elphaba, the Wicked Witch of the West. During Elphaba's show-stopping song "Defying Gravity," she flies for the first time by defying the forces and limits that threaten to bring her down. She literally defies gravity, but the song is really about the challenge of resisting the rules and limits that weigh us down and prevent us from soaring. Just as gravity is an invisible force that influences us every moment even though we generally don't think about it, our minds are subject to outside forces and influences that are as unseen and powerful as gravity. Modern aviation changed the world because it allowed us to defy an unseen force that had always limited us—it allowed us to fly. If you want to soar spiritually, you are going to need to learn how to defy the "gravity" that weighs down your mind without you even knowing it's at work.

We like to think that we're in control of our thoughts and emotions, but so many things influence us, often without our awareness or permission. If you want to build a bulletproof mind, you need to become aware of the way that your mental habits currently undermine your resiliency. Let's try to uncover how your mind got built in the first place so we can see what we're dealing with.

Becoming an Interior Designer

Think about the house or apartment you grew up living in. Now think about the space you currently inhabit. If you're like most people, your style and preferences are different from your parents', at least to some degree. What kind of music do you like? Is it different from the music your parents listened to? Most of us have found our own favorite musical styles or artists, right? There aren't many women who want to dress like their mothers, and the perennial advertising phrase "Not your father's (fill in the blank—car, radio, investment fund)" speaks volumes about our desire to find our own way. With all the independence we exhibit through our choices in the material world, our inner world may not be completely our own. When you were born, you were a fresh slate. Then, as you developed, your parents, siblings, and the culture around you began to program your mind to think, feel, and respond in certain ways. If you were exceptionally lucky, your early programming prepared you to deal with adversity and crisis in ways that allowed you to come out on top of any challenge. More likely, your early programming actually undermined your innate resilience and made it harder for you to negotiate life's hurdles. Whatever kind of programming you were exposed to, the important thing to begin thinking about is that you are probably still running those programs whether they work for you or not. Spiritually speaking, this is the equivalent of sitting on plastic slipcovers and listening to music on eight-track tapes. For most of us, there are better ways to live inside our minds, and spiritually bulletproof people make it their business to create mental habitats that really assist them in living their best lives. Building a bulletproof mind requires you to act as your *own* "interior designer"; you must consciously create new and positive ways for your mind to respond to crisis, heartbreak, or adversity. Here are a couple of examples of "programs" that our minds might still be running just because they are our default setting:

- Maybe you've heard really negative and defeatist *words* related to any kind of crisis or adversity. You may have been programmed to respond to any of life's hits with verbal expressions like *I can't believe this is happening to me* or *It's not fair!* Maybe you grew up hearing phrases like *It's one thing after another!* or *I can't take any more!* One man we worked with frequently used the expression "This is bullshit!" when describing the various challenges and issues in his life; it turned out that his father stomped around the house saying the same thing about any problem he faced.

- Maybe you saw really negative responses to adversity, stress, or heartbreak. Perhaps you grew up in a house where people ran away when things got tough or where people went into denial and refused to face or talk about anything negative. Maybe you saw people drink or escape into other addictions when faced with a hit.

When you don't have good models for overcoming adversity, it is difficult, indeed, to take a hit and come out on top. Your own responses to crisis may be modeled on these behaviors you saw. Your spirit needs better models! When facing a serious trial, words and thoughts like these undermine your mind's ability to respond optimally to the situation. While it is certainly okay to have thoughts or say words that are negative, it is important to find new ways of responding to crisis that move you toward a more positive outcome. A steady diet of negative thinking and talking makes it almost impossible to bounce back after a hit. Your spirit needs better food!

We Interrupt This Program . . .

It's really important to acknowledge that your "programming" affects your thoughts and responses. This is especially true when you've taken a hit because when you're in crisis, you're much more likely to regress and act from old patterns. When you realize the impact that your early programming has on your spiritual resiliency, you'll want to give yourself the gift of reprogramming your mind so that it can better assist you. The good news is that your mind is an evolving and brilliant tool that has a built-in mechanism for self-improvement. The human brain is "plastic," or adaptable, throughout life and this works in your favor. You *can* build a bulletproof mind. All of the secrets in this book will work to help you think about and respond to adversity in a positive way, but the next step is to learn a few little thinking habits that will allow your mind to reprogram itself more quickly and more easily.

• • •

Bounce Back Boot Camp

Here are a few techniques for you to try. If you practice them in a disciplined way on a daily basis, you will turbo-charge your transformation by harnessing the power of your mind.

- Practice "thought-stopping." This is a simple little strategy for replacing ineffective programming. Get conscious about your thoughts and words. When you think about or discuss a hit you've taken, pay careful attention to the words in your mind or coming out of your mouth—notice the pattern of your reactions. Every time you have a thought that doesn't serve your new bulletproof mind—one that reveals a no-longer-useful pattern of thinking about adversity— stop yourself and say something like "Cancel that!" aloud. One woman we know literally puts her hand up the way she would if she wanted to stop a person walking toward her and tells the unwanted thought to "Stop right there!" This may seem goofy to you at first, but if you stick with it, you will slowly but surely get rid of programming that undermines your resilient mind.
- Learn how to "reframe." This little habit helps you replace thoughts or language that doesn't help with new mental images or words that will feed your mind what it needs to support you through any adversity. When you cancel a thought or spoken idea, immediately replace it with a more affirming and healthy substitute. For example, if you have the thought "I don't think I can ever get over this," stop the thought and then replace it with something like "I believe that I can heal from this and I will seek the support I need to do so." It is definitely cumbersome and awkward to consistently "reframe" your thoughts and words, but with repetition, you will be amazed at how quickly you find yourself needing to do it less and less.

- Imagine that you are walking behind yourself. Cultivate a part of yourself that stands behind the thinking/talking/acting self and observes and directs. Begin to think of this aspect of yourself as your spirit. Know that your spirit is wise and resilient beyond measure and practice accepting its coaching throughout the day.

- Remember that building a bulletproof mind is not something that you just do once and then coast on forever. It's more like going to the chiropractor—you need to keep making small adjustments to keep yourself aligned. It's a kind of maintenance that you do as a gift to yourself and your bulletproof spirit.

•　•　•

Bullets Are Really Spiritual Bullion

In the middle of difficulty lies opportunity.

—ALBERT EINSTEIN

SPIRITUALLY FRAGILE PEOPLE BELIEVE THAT THE PHYSICAL, EMO-
tional, and financial hits they take are completely worthless and
wasteful—and they bitterly resent them. Spiritually bulletproof
people know that life's heartbreaking hits always contain the seeds
of life's soul-making moments, and they see them as incredibly
valuable, even if they are downright devastating. Where spiritually vulnerable people are quick to judge a hit as being a total
loss, their more resilient counterparts resist despair because deep
down they believe that there is treasure lying somewhere beneath
the ruins all around them and they're willing to look for it.

Looking for treasure where others see only worthless rubble
is an ancient tradition that we would be well-served to revive.
Alchemy is the ancient art and science concerned with turning
base metals into gold. Alchemy also refers to transformation in

general. Jean Dubuis, a French philosopher and one of the world's renowned modern-day alchemists, writes that "Alchemy is the art of manipulating life, and consciousness in matter, to help it evolve, or to solve problems of inner disharmonies." *Spiritual* alchemy is all about the transformation of our souls—finding the treasure within, even *creating* it out of devastation and loss. While they are certainly not immune to the heartbreaks that life hands out, spiritually bulletproof people consciously undertake the art of spiritual alchemy—they work to uncover the spiritual gold hidden inside the hardest hits.

> Spiritually bulletproof people consciously undertake the art of spiritual alchemy— they work to uncover the spiritual gold hidden inside the hardest hits.

Like many secrets contained in this book, this one is about seeing in a new way. Coming out on top of a loss or a tragedy requires us to *transform* the way we think about adversity, suffering, and crisis. Where does this transformation begin? Back in the Middle Ages, it was common for alchemists to use skulls as the vessels for their chemical experiments. Though this might seem a bit creepy to our modern sensibilities, the reason for this was deeply symbolic. The skull is the receptacle for the mind— and the mind is where all transformation originates. Before any change appears in the material world, it first must manifest in our minds. This perspective can be cultivated and will help you begin your journey back to your own bulletproof spirit.

We Shall See . . .

Referring to the environmental crisis, Al Gore says "We sometimes emphasize the danger in a crisis without focusing on the opportunities that are there." This perspective is found in the wisdom traditions of many cultures. The Chinese create the word "crisis" with two characters, one meaning "danger" and the other meaning "opportunity." There is an old Chinese story about the dual nature of crisis or adversity:

> *One day, a farmer was working in his rice paddy when a horse wandered onto his land. When no owner followed, the farmer brought the horse home and fed and watered him. His neighbors, hearing of his coup, rushed over that evening with congratulations on his good luck at finding such a prized animal to help him with his work. No matter what felicitations came his way, the farmer would only say "We shall see . . ."*
>
> *The next day, his only son—a strapping young man and the apple of his eye—took the horse out to the plains and rode him hard. The horse stepped on a snake and threw the youth, causing him to break his leg. Hearing of this terrible blow, the farmer's neighbors gathered around him with condolences about this unlucky turn of events. Again, the farmer would only reply "We shall see . . ."*
>
> *The following week, a warlord from a neighboring region stormed through the village and took with him all the men of fighting age. Laid up with a broken leg, the farmer's son was the only young man left behind to survive what ended up being a suicidal mission. Once more, the villagers came by to congratulate the farmer on his good fortune, but by now they knew that all he would say about the situation was "We shall see . . ."*

Now, the story goes on like this for many twists and turns of what we would call good or bad fortune. Never does the farmer conclude anything about the events he faces other than his "We shall see" response. This classic Chinese tale illustrates an ancient wisdom tradition found in many cultures but now widely forgotten—it points to the human habit of judging events or circumstances with our limited perspective rather than remembering the truth that all events play out into a much larger context than is apparent in the moment. The farmer symbolizes the wise part of our minds that remembers when tragedy or misfortune strikes to say "We shall see."

Spiritually bulletproof people either innately or consciously adopt this "We shall see" way of thinking about the hits they take throughout their lives. If necessary, they reorient themselves and reframe their perspectives to keep this attitude when it is most difficult to do so. Spiritually vulnerable people often make the mistake of assuming that what appears on the surface of a situation is all there is to it. They forget to look deeper and this makes it very difficult to weather or bounce back from adversity. The reason why spiritually bulletproof people are able to keep saying "We shall see" is, in large part, because they intuit (and have come to trust that intuition through experience) that, despite all outward appearances, bullets really *are* bullion, or gold. To know this in theory is one thing, but to keep this perspective when you've taken a heartbreaking hit is the goal.

A Golden Opportunity

Bernie Siegel is a Yale-trained physician and the author of *Love, Medicine & Miracles* and many other books and resources for people living with cancer and other chronic illnesses. One thread that runs through much of his work is the relationship he's observed between attitude and healing. His books and online resources share story after story about people who have taken devastating hits and come out on top. Bernie believes that people he calls "exceptional cancer patients" exhibit attitudes, beliefs, and behaviors that influence their healing. One core trait he points to throughout his work is the ability to find the good or the gift in the struggle one faces. He writes about patients he's known who actually say that cancer is the best thing that's ever happened to them!

It is true that spiritually bulletproof people possess a willingness—even an eagerness—to go for the gold. The situations they face and the hits they take are no different from anyone else's, but their attitudes make all the difference. In a sense, it is quite simple: Spiritually resilient people make it a point to *look* for the valuable lesson, the treasure of new awareness, or the riches of love they find when they dig through the muck. Abraham Lincoln believed that "Most folks are about as happy as they make up their minds to be," and when you make up your mind to be happy, it's much easier to do if you can believe that there's gold in those hills of heartache.

Rejecting the Gold Standard

These first few chapters are asking a lot of you, but they will begin to work a kind of magic in you if you can have faith and just try to think a little differently. We've had many workshop participants and clients over the years who were really resistant to any suggestion that there could be anything even a *little* bit good about the hits they had taken. And we really do understand where they were coming from. Please realize that we're not saying that there is anything good *about* the bad things that happen—we're suggesting that good can come *from* the hits we take. This is a very important distinction. It is natural and understandable to rebel against the idea that you're supposed to think that something so *bad* can contain anything remotely *good*. Here are some common reasons that keep people from going for the gold:

- You might believe that to open your mind up to the possibility of finding the treasure buried under the ruins of your hit would be somehow working against your own best interests. On some level, you may believe that to find value in your crisis or loss would be to invalidate what you have gone through.
- You may think that trying to create gold from the wreckage of your hit would be to let people off the hook or condone something that just isn't right.

- You might find yourself thinking that this kind of spiritual alchemy is a kind of denial or you might think it sounds like you'd just be fooling yourself.
- You genuinely may not be able to believe that anything good or valuable could ever come out of the hit you've taken. You might think that if it's not apparent to you now, it never will be.
- You may enjoy the sympathy you get because of the hit you've taken (which is only natural, by the way) and fear that to begin to see differently would take some of that support away from you.

All of these reasons for feeling resistant make sense when you're hurting or angry. We ask that you trust us enough to *try* some new ways of seeing and being in your mind and in the world. We know intimately the challenge of spiritual alchemy and can attest to its power to heal you. When I came home from the midwife visit where I learned that I was carrying a dead baby, I *literally* kept repeating the words "We shall see." I said them over and over as an affirmation of what I had come to know was true from years of spiritual work and facing adversity in my life. There was certainly nothing remotely good or golden about what I was experiencing, but I trusted that somehow, in some way that was completely unclear to me at that moment, something valuable might come from all of the heartache and loss I was going through. And though it took years for me to dig through the rubble and find the treasure waiting for me, the belief that bullets really are bullion was like a small raft in a turbulent sea—it was something for me to hold onto. And sometimes, that is enough.

You might have to pass through many stages before you're ready to look for buried treasure. In the days and weeks and months after Azim's son was murdered, it was all he could do to keep living. But eventually, after grieving and moving through other necessary stages of healing, Azim began to consider the idea that in the most heartbreaking of hits were also found the seeds of life's soul-making moments. Being willing to try to transmute pain and suffering into something beautiful and of value is at the heart of Azim's ability to take the worst hit imaginable and come out on top.

Starting today, begin to consider that the hit you've taken may contain treasure hiding underneath layers of pain, time, and healing. It will be there when you're ready to start digging.

• • •

Bounce Back Boot Camp

Try these strategies and suggestions to help you uncover the riches inherent in your challenging circumstances:

- Make a list of any hits you have taken or are currently dealing with. Make sure that you include hits from earlier in your life. When you are done listing, take a few moments to meditate on each of these "bullets" you took. Can you now, with the perspective that time brings, find any buried treasure among the ruins of these hardships? For each hit, try to find some gold that emerged from the ashes. When one of my clients tried this activity, she realized that one of the worst hits she'd taken—growing up with alcoholic and abusive parents—actually gave her some of the greatest gifts she felt she'd ever received. She came to see that most of the things she now cherished in her life (her wonderful relationship with her own children, her work as a therapist, and her close and authentic friendships) emerged because of the lessons she had received through growing up the way she did.

- Many times, the treasure we seek is found along the path of service. Begin to consider the idea that you might not be the only person involved in the equation. Maybe there are riches for you to share with others as a result of the hit you've taken. In Azim's case, reaching out to help others by sharing his story and experience was the beginning of his own journey toward coming out on top of the most devastating loss. What value do you now know or have to give that might benefit others? Use your journal to brainstorm about possibilities of service to others.

- Wear a piece of gold jewelry (it can be costume jewelry!) every day as a symbol of your commitment to finding the bullion behind the bullet. It can even be something like a money clip, as long as it's something you will see throughout the day. One man we knew didn't like to wear jewelry, so he tied a simple piece of gold string around his wrist. Like most shifts in perception, this one is easier to master if you give yourself cues to remind yourself of your new perspective.

• • •

A Bullet Is a Spiritual Bridge

Problems are not stop signs, they're guidelines.
—Rev. Robert H. Schuller

SPIRITUALLY FRAGILE PEOPLE BELIEVE THAT THE BAD THINGS THAT happen to them are things that get in the way of or detour them away from what they really want. They look at heartbreaking hits and all they can see are roadblocks and stop signs. Spiritually bulletproof people look at these same outwardly unfortunate or even devastating circumstances and see them for what they really are: bridges that, once crossed, will lead them to a place that has the potential to fulfill their hearts' deepest desires or that is connected to their lives' truest purpose.

John Pierpont Morgan, American financier, banker, and philanthropist, believed that "The wise man bridges the gap by means of which he can get from where he is to where he wants to go." J. P. Morgan is referring here to the necessity of making our *own* bridges where none appear for us, and he became one of the wealthiest men in the world by building his own bridges of opportunity wherever he went. If you want to reap the rich emotional rewards that come from super spiritual resiliency, you too will need to learn how to build your own bridges—ones that will lead you from the hits you take to the rewards on the other side.

> Spiritually bulletproof people learn to find or, if necessary, build the bridges that will take them from heartbreaking hit to the happiness and destiny that awaits them.

Knowing that happiness has a habit of hanging around on the other side of heartache, spiritually bulletproof people learn to find or, if necessary, build the bridges that will take them from heartbreaking hit to the happiness and destiny that awaits them.

Although these are the kind of bridges that you will need to find or build yourself, it is important to remember that you follow in the footsteps of the great men and women who have come before you. No matter how many or how few years have passed since then, each of us has ancestors who built their own bridges between an old world and a new one. André Gide, a French author who won the Nobel Prize for literature, writes that "One does not discover new lands without consenting to lose sight of the shore for a very long time." Keep clear in your mind that you truly do walk in the shadows of men and women who built their own bridges across the oceans and the seas, the deserts and the mountains. Never forget that though you often must cross a bridge by yourself, you never walk alone.

Chasing Rainbows

In many Native American traditions, the rainbow is a prominent symbol in art and myth. A Navajo song tells the generations to "Walk on a rainbow trail. . . . There is a way out of every dark mist, over a rainbow trail." If you think about it, a rainbow is a magnificent bridge reaching from heaven all the way down to us here on earth. The rainbow as a symbol resonates across cultures and through time.

In the Old Testament of the Bible the rainbow is an important symbol in the story of Noah and his ark. The rainbow is alluded to as a symbol of God's covenant with Noah, a sign that God would always be with us. The rainbow is also a prominent dream symbol. Dr. Clarissa Pinkola Estés, poet, psychoanalyst, and author of *Women Who Run with the Wolves: Myths and Stories of the Wild Woman Archetype* and many other books and articles, writes:

> *One of the oldest mythos containing the symbol of the bridge, is that of the "Rainbow Bridge," a Native American religious symbol, that speaks of a way of life, a way of living wherein one stands between the destroyed world and the new world.*

Spiritually fragile people focus all of their attention on the "destroyed world," not thinking about the "new world" that is on the other side of any hardship. Therefore, any "bullets" they take make them frustrated, resentful, or even despondent. Spiritually bulletproof people are only human, and they, too, can have temporary negative feelings about the difficult things that come their way. One very important difference that *makes* all the difference for them is that resilient people quickly reframe the hits they take as bridges that are showing them the way to where they want or need to go. Their attention goes quickly and in a concerted way toward the "new world" that awaits them over the bridge.

Somewhere over the Rainbow

Most people do not like change. It is natural to want to keep things the same in your life, and going over a bridge to a new world you never particularly wanted to discover might not be all that appealing to you. Most of us choose to find or build our bridges only when we're standing at the edge of a "destroyed world"—an unraveling relationship, a lost job, or a body facing serious illness. J.C., a young woman we worked with, lost her athletic scholarship to a top college when a serious knee injury took her out of competitive sports for good. Her whole life up until that point was built around her physical talents and all her friends were teammates and athletes. She was heartbroken and felt as if she were losing everything. Through working together with some of the secrets in this book, she began to see that the "bullet" she took was really a bridge to a place she wouldn't have thought to visit but that she began to understand was part of her destiny. She had also always been very interested in spirituality, but her grueling practice and workout schedule made it almost impossible for her to delve into these interests. Well, J.C. graduated from college and went on to the seminary to become an Episcopalian priest. She says with deep conviction that she has found her true calling but that without the "bullet" she took, she might never have slowed down enough to hear that call.

When you're looking into the abyss, hovering between what no longer is and something new that you can't yet imagine, begin to consider the possibility of a "rainbow bridge" or a "rainbow trail" that has come into being expressly for you at the moment you need it. And if you can't see any rainbows, begin to consider that you're looking in the wrong place. Turn your attention inward to where the real action is. Maybe *somewhere over the rainbow* is really somewhere inside of you.

Bridging the Gap

Bridge to Terabithia, by Katherine Paterson, won the Newbery Medal for children's literature in 1978, and in 2007 was made into a very successful movie. It is the story of two lonely kids, Jesse and Leslie, who create a magical kingdom in the forest. It is a story about the power of friendship and imagination in helping us become who we are meant to be, but it is also a story about love and loss. The only way to get to Terabithia is by using a rope to swing over the creek that separates the magical kingdom from the known territory. When Leslie drowns while trying to go to Terabithia on her own one day, Jesse must somehow come to terms with this heartbreaking hit. He decides to build a bridge to Terabithia, and it is through the building of this bridge that he begins to heal from his loss and find the new horizons that are his destiny. This story speaks to the hearts of children and adults who read it because its symbolism resonates with what we know to be true. Just as Terabithia is a place inside the minds of the characters and the bridge symbolizes the characters' commitment to live fully in the imaginative mind, the happiness we can find on the other side of a loss can only be accessed if we are willing to see the "bullets" we take as bridges that beckon us to a new world waiting to be discovered. To see bullets as bridges requires bravery and boldness. It asks that we see with the eyes of imagination. It challenges us to look inside when searching for the place we're headed.

Bridging the gap often means leaving things, people, or situations behind as we find our new circumstances. Many times a bullet is a kind of bridge that asks us to look inward to identify our true desires and to muster the strength to let go of our superficial ones. Most of the people we've worked with over the years have had some version of the same experience: They either chose or were forced to let go of some aspect of their lives, and in so doing, were able to find some new part of themselves or way of living in the world that was more authentic. Often, clues about how to build your bridge or where it's leading are built into the hit you've taken. Sometimes, the hints we need to bridge the gap between the old and new worlds are hiding in the middle of our hardest challenges. Some of the time, these clues are connected with a lesson we need or that we're finally ready to learn and integrate. When there is a gap between what we know and what we need to know or who we are and who we need to be that must be spanned, the bullets we take may be the very opportunity we need to get up to speed.

Destiny Is Calling

The bridges hidden in hardships ultimately go to good places. They may bring you somewhere you never wanted to go and they may take you into uncharted territory, but they always, *always* lead to a higher ground inside of you. There are changes we need to make and journeys we need to take that apathy and fear would dissuade us from considering. The blessing of the hits we take is that, seen and responded to properly, they can propel us out of that apathy and through that fear. The sheer force of a hit can push us right over a bridge we would never have crossed in a million years if left to our own devices. Your bulletproof spirit will help you find or build these bridges and invites you to seek the destiny that waits on the other side.

• • •

Bounce Back Boot Camp

Here are some suggestions for bridging the gap between heartache and happiness:

- Hang a prism in one of your windows. A prism is a glass ornament that creates a little rainbow when the sunlight shines through it. Reflect upon the rainbow and its symbolism—use it as a visual reminder to "walk on the rainbow trail."
- Use your journal to brainstorm about the bullet or bullets you've taken and how they might really be bridges of a sort. Where has the hit you've taken led you that you might never have gone on your own? Where have you journeyed to inside of yourself because of the heartache or challenge you've had to handle?
- Consider creating a "Bridging Ceremony" for yourself.

Make a symbolic "bridge" using materials convenient to you. You can make a "bridge" from a rainbow of colored ribbons laid out on your living-room floor or you can pretend that a log in your backyard is a bridge. A double row of votive candles can be arranged like a bridge to walk through. Be creative—perhaps your "bridge" can somehow symbolize the hit you've taken and your journey past it. One client took his divorce papers and laid them in a row on his back deck. Once you have your "bridge" in place, take some time to meditate on your willingness to cross the bridge from your hit to the happiness waiting for you on the other side. When you're ready, cross over the bridge you've made. Take some quiet time to process what thoughts, feelings, and ideas arise for you. Pay attention to any flashes of insight or intuition. Even if nothing comes clear for you, know that your ceremony sends a powerful signal inward to your unconscious mind and outward into the universe that you're ready and willing to bridge the gap.

• • •

Hits Are What It's All About

*Only through experience of trial and suffering can the soul
be strengthened, ambition inspired, and success achieved.*

—HELEN KELLER

SPIRITUALLY BULLETPROOF PEOPLE UNDERSTAND THAT, NO MATTER
how things seem on the surface, heartbreak and loss are integral
parts of the universe's benevolent unfolding. The key word here
is *integral*—bullets are *built into* the very fabric of life, and they are
an essential element of the human experience and *not*, as many
people believe, an aberration from the normal course of events.
They are as necessary to the wholeness of life as are blessings—
resilient people understand that hits are not just the things that get
in the way of "real life"; they are really what life is all about.
Spiritually fragile people are often shocked and resentful when
life disappoints them. But expecting to go through life without
facing serious hurdles or heartbreaks is like trying to play football and not get tackled—it ain't happenin'.

We live in a culture that dislikes messiness. Modern science, medicine, and technology convince us that there's an answer for every question and a solution for every problem. Spiritually bullet-proof people are as optimistic and positive as anyone (in fact, they are generally more so), but they also accept that suffering is part of the human condition be-cause they see the growth and development that usually accom-panies it as vital. They trust the wisdom of the universe and know that losses and crises serve a powerful purpose in our lives. On a very basic level, spiritually resilient people believe that it's *okay* that hits happen. They may not like what they have to face and they certainly try to dodge bullets whenever possible, but resilient people also accept that taking hits is part of why we're here. Though no one *wants* to ex-perience the suffering or difficulty that comes with the trials life hands out, spiritually bulletproof people expect to take serious hits and believe that these hits are essential to a purposeful life.

> Spiritually bulletproof people expect to take serious hits and believe that these hits are essential to a purposeful life.

You might find this perspective difficult to consider right now, but it's important to remember that you are in the process of transforming how you respond to adversity. You are breaking through barriers and limits that have, up until now, kept you from tapping into the full power of your own bulletproof spirit.

Most of the limits we experience are self-imposed. Poet William Blake called these limits "mind-forged manacles" be-cause they originate only in our perception of what's possible or not. Often, when we see that a certain thing is *possible* because someone else is doing it, we begin to realize that our limits are illusions that we, too, can break past. For example, before Roger Bannister ran the mile in less than four minutes in 1954, no one had ever been able to do so. Since then, countless runners have gone on to break that record. Bannister broke more than a record with his famous race—he also broke a psychological barrier for others who followed. Being able to take a hit and come out on top, like most of life's challenges, is a kind of "head game." Super spiritual resilience requires you to break through certain psychological barriers. It can be hard to see life from a bulletproof point of view if your family modeled less-than-ideal responses to adversity. It can also be difficult to see hits in this way if you buy into the myth of seamless perfection that Madison Avenue and Hollywood depict. It may be necessary for you to find new models to help you tap into your bulletproof spirit. It's no accident that you are holding these secrets in your hands at this moment—take a moment to remind yourself that you are connecting with new models right now. There are plenty of spiritually bulletproof people whose responses to adversity have broken through psychological barriers we all face. Azim's life was *literally* ripped apart by an actual bullet. Losing his son to a real-life bullet only convinced him more thoroughly that the hits we take are an essential, albeit painful, element of a purposeful life.

The Only Game in Town

Most people are so caught up in the busyness and challenges of daily life that they do not often stop and think about the *purpose* of life. Thinking about the meaning of life kicks up very big questions that we're usually content to leave to philosophers, theologians, and artists—most of us are kept quite occupied just getting through the day. When things are going fine, it's easy to take life at face value and avoid the really tough, soul-searching questions. But there's nothing like a heartbreaking hit to make us question the meaning of our lives and our suffering. Some of the worst suffering we've seen clients go through was existential in nature—wondering what the hell their lives were about and feeling like nothing made sense. For most people, existential or spiritual anguish is actually more painful than physical suffering. When we can't find meaning in what is happening to us, it is easy to slip into despair when we take a hit.

One major advantage that spiritually bulletproof people have is that they know the game they're playing, so life's struggles have a different meaning for them than for most people. In the most basic terms, resilient people think that life is like a giant bumper-car ride—they buckle up and *expect* to get hit. To them, bumping up against other people, difficult circumstances, or devastating events is not only inevitable, it is actually *desirable;* they understand that the hits they take help them to become their fullest selves and they also believe that personal or spiritual evolution is central to the purpose of life. Obviously, this doesn't mean that they go out looking for trouble or heartache; they simply live their lives with heightened awareness of the role that adversity plays in their own development.

Dr. Cherie Carter-Scott, author of *If Life Is a Game, These Are the Rules,* believes that we will each be presented with lessons that are custom-designed for us and designed to teach us what we need to learn next. She teaches that these lessons often come in the form of painful events or situations. According to Dr. Carter-Scott, these lessons are different for each person and they are completely inevitable—they are one of the rules of play in this game we call life. In our work, we've observed that spiritually bulletproof people intuit or consciously acknowledge this part of life's game plan, though they might not use the same language to describe it.

Chasing Tigers

There's an old Zen story that speaks to the value of life's hardships:

A man was walking through a field when a tiger sprang at him from the brush and began to chase him. The man ran for his life but was no match for the tiger and, in desperation, he jumped off the cliff at the edge of the field to escape certain death. As he jumped, he happened to catch hold of a vine that kept him dan-

gling against the cliff wall a hundred feet above the ground below. When he looked up, he saw that the tiger was prowling the edge of the cliff ten feet above him, and when he looked down, he saw that there was another tiger waiting below. He held on as hard as he could, praying that he could wait them both out. To make matters worse, he spotted two little mice gnawing at the vine that held him and he knew that it could break at any time. Just then, he saw a single strawberry growing out of a crevice in the side of the cliff just within his reach. Hanging on with one hand, he reached out and picked the strawberry and ate it. Never had anything tasted so sweet.

This story reveals a secret known by spiritually bulletproof people: If you want to really live with purpose, you must understand the value of tigers. The beauty, joy, and sweetness of life symbolized by the strawberry are always there to be noticed and enjoyed, but without the crisis represented by the tigers, we would most likely fail to value it. Learning to see the value of life's strawberries is common sense. Learning to see the value of life's tigers is true wisdom. If you want to turbo-charge your spiritual resiliency, begin to consider that tigers and strawberries are really what life's all about—everything else is just filler.

The Real Reason for Relationships

If you want to tap into your bulletproof spirit, it's important to think about other people and your relationships a little differently. Jean-Paul Sartre's famous line, "Hell is other people," has it half right. Hell may be other people, but so is heaven. Other people are almost always at the heart of our most heartbreaking hits and our greatest happiness. Even financial or career hits usually end up being about the people or relationships connected to the money or job. For example, when Harold, a machinist in his fifties, was fired with no cause, no explanation, no notice, and no severance pay or benefits after more than twenty years of faithful service to the small company he had helped the owner build from the ground up, he was hurt, angry, and in shock. Of course, with a family to provide for and few good prospects for a similar position in a tight regional economy, he was worried about the financial toll of the hit he had taken. But much more devastating to him was the emotional blow of being treated so heartlessly by a man he considered a friend as much as an employer. While Harold ended up finding a better position very quickly, it took him much longer to rebound from the damage to a relationship he valued. Relationships, including the ones we have with ourselves, really are at the heart of all we experience as heaven or hell here on earth.

Relationships serve many purposes in our lives—they comfort us, inspire us, challenge us, and help us accomplish things we couldn't do on our own. But above and beyond all these purposes, human relationships are the best vehicles available to us for our spiritual journeys. The most compelling, though usually hidden, reason for relationships is that they provide the fuel for the adversity that forges our finest selves. A scripture from the Book of Proverbs tells us "As iron sharpens iron, so one man sharpens another." Other people make us into better people, if we can come out on top of the hits we take through our relationships with them. Our relationships are like the other cars on the bumper-car ride of life—without them, there would be nothing to bump up *against* and the ride would have no meaning. It would certainly not give us the friction we need to polish our personalities and souls—with nothing to rub up against or abrade us, we would stay spiritually jagged throughout our lives. It is as if we are diamonds in the rough—without the tumbler of relationships or the laser of painful challenges, there'd be nothing to shape us or cut us into the polished gems that we're meant to become over the course of our time here together.

Spiritually bulletproof people understand that the universe teaches us the lessons we're meant to learn through the relationships we participate in. We're all here bumping into each other, hurting each other, and getting hurt, and resilient people tend to take all the bumping much less personally than do spiritually fragile people. They also recognize that though teams form and then change sides, opponents face off and then move on to new adversaries, the game always stays the same. The names, places, and circumstances keep changing, but the bumping into each other never ends. Spiritually bulletproof people are more comfortable on this ride than their more fragile counterparts because they have a deep, unshakable sense that we're all on the same team. If you want to connect with your own bulletproof spirit, begin to look at all of your relationships and their attendant problems and crises—at home, at work, with casual acquaintances, and even with adversaries—as opportunities to become your best self. Other people are only in your life to help you learn more about yourself, and the hits you take because of them are what life is all about. The more you can realign yourself to this reality when things get tough, the closer you'll get to the essence of your own bulletproof spirit.

* * *

Bounce Back Boot Camp

Here are some suggestions for appreciating the hits you take as part of the game of life:

- Spend some time in a place where you find it easy to contemplate things. Natural places like the beach or the woods can be excellent contemplative environments. Maybe try a church, temple, or mosque when no services are being held. We've had clients who swore that their cars were perfect places to think without distraction. Never underestimate the power of a cemetery to get you thinking about what really matters. Bring your journal and spend some time exploring your ideas about the purpose of life. Jot down any thoughts you have on the subject—don't worry if they don't sound right or if you're confused. After free-writing for a while, respond in writing to the following prompt: *The hits I've taken are connected to my life's purpose because* . . . Write as little or as much as comes naturally.

- Make a list of the hits you've taken that have impacted you the most. Think about each of these hits and decide if a relationship is at the heart of the matter. (Don't discount the relationship you have with yourself.) What did bumping up against each of these people teach you about yourself?

- If you have the chance, get yourself on a bumper-car ride. You'll never look at bumper cars in quite the same way again. Let the wise child who still lives inside you remember the truth about life and its hits.

•   •   •

Recognize Your "Realationships"

Problems can become opportunities when the right people come together.

—ROBERT REDFORD

IF YOU WANT TO TAP INTO THE FULL POWER OF YOUR BULLETPROOF spirit, you need to be able to recognize the real role that relationships play in your life. If you carry around illusions or erroneous expectations about the bonds and interactions you have with other people, it is unlikely that you'll be able to bounce back from the hits you'll inevitably take in your various relationships. Spiritually bulletproof people understand that the most important reason why other people are in our lives is to help us learn more about ourselves and so that we can do the same for them.

The Greek philosopher Epicurus believed that "You don't develop courage by being happy in your relationships every day. You develop it by surviving difficult times and challenging adversity." People with super spiritual resiliency consciously reframe their connections with other people as perfect vehicles for spiritual and personal growth and this helps them to handle the heartbreaking hits and inevitable challenges that accompany all human interactions. Though they find deep happiness and meaning in their bonds with other people, spiritually bulletproof people see past the surface dynamics of their relationships to their real role: mutual spiritual evolution.

> Spiritually bulletproof people see past the surface dynamics of their relationships to their real role: mutual spiritual evolution.

But this doesn't mean that they don't have the same conflicts, problems, and heartbreaks that we all have. Resilient people are often the quintessential "people who need people," and they experience at least as much interpersonal drama as others do. A critical difference is that they instinctively or consciously view these dramas and the people attached to them as the ultimate teachers in their lives. They completely accept a central tenet of spiritual resiliency: Other people are in our lives and we're in theirs so that we can all learn more about ourselves and become more of who we're meant to be.

"Realationship" 101

Think about the various relationships you participate in. You may maintain many close bonds with family and friends or maybe you have a smaller circle of people in your life. If you stop and think about it for a minute, you probably have relationships with more people than you realize. You may live with people or near people, work with few or many people, shop or do errands near or in the businesses of others, have conflicts or misunderstandings with folks, and have people in your life who live far away but are always on your mind in one way or another. There are many levels of relationships, from casual acquaintance to deeply intimate romantic partner. There are relationships that provide mostly pleasure and that are relatively easy to maintain, and there are relationships that create a lot of conflict and pain in our lives or that are more difficult to keep. Each relationship offers different rewards and requires different care and effort. Each relationship is an entity unto itself—it's something created when two people come together that is completely new under the sun. If you want to be spiritually bulletproof, begin to consider that each of these relationships presents you with an extremely valuable and unique opportunity to evolve in the direction of your highest good.

One of the most interesting (and exasperating) aspects of this truth is that it is often the most difficult relationships that teach us the most. Spiritually fragile people see their difficult relationships as the bane of their existence and resent them, but more resilient people recognize them as their most powerful opportunities to grow and learn. You might read these words and think "Okay, I agree with all this in theory, but you don't know my (mother, brother, father-in-law, neighbor, boss, ex-husband, you-fill-in-the-blank) and have no idea what I go through." And you may be right—each situation is different and there *are* relationships that are so destructive that the only personal growth they should inspire is learning how to end them. But overall, most of our relationships deserve being elevated to *"realationship"* status; we should give them credit for being the truest and most profound teachers we'll ever have in this school of life.

Resistance Training

Napoleon Hill's famous book *Think and Grow Rich* is one of the best-selling books of all time. This personal-success guru believed that "The path of least resistance makes all rivers, and some men, crooked," and it is certainly true that without relationships that push us in some way, we are denying ourselves the straightest path to personal growth. Carl Jung believed that "What we resist persists," and spiritually bulletproof people pay serious attention to people or relationships that create internal resistance because they know that feelings of resistance are important clues about where we need to develop next. They also rightly understand that our feelings of resistance to certain people or relationships tell us more about ourselves than they do about other people. Spiritually resilient people work with their own feelings of resistance in relationships and are humble enough to believe that those feelings are there to teach them lessons they need to learn.

Spiritually resilient people do the hard work of sifting through and honestly examining their resistance to other people. This is easiest to do when the stakes are low and the relationship is casual. Consider the case of Alexis, a woman who came up and introduced herself when I was grocery shopping with my three kids one day last summer. Alexis approached me as I was loading my bags into the back of my station wagon and said something like "I saw you shopping inside and I couldn't believe how calm, cool, and collected you were with your three little kids in a crowded food store. You smiled the whole time and nothing ruffled you. What's your secret?" We started chatting, and she revealed that when she first spotted me wheeling around the store with a balloon-toting toddler in tow, she noticed that she felt a lot of resistance toward me. She basically found it annoying that I could, in her words, "do it all." She couldn't help it, she said—it just irritated her that I could shop efficiently, enjoy my children, be nice, and chat up the check-out clerk all while looking, in her words, "perky and put-together." She confessed that she had hoped to find out that I was a nanny instead of a mommy. (And I confessed that she had caught me on a good day!) After more chatting, I found out that Alexis was a new mother who still was adjusting to the whole crazy juggling act of motherhood and had barely stopped nursing. I reassured Alexis that everything she saw in me and that she thought was some kind of "secret" was already inside her just waiting to unfold. We had a great talk and I gave her my card. Well, months later she contacted me because she had written an article that was being published that was a reflection on our meeting. In it, she shared that our meeting at the grocery store was a turning point for her because she had paid attention to her initial resistance to me and asked herself some important questions. It turns out that Alexis felt as though she had lost touch with the parts of herself that she saw in me. She was experiencing what many new mothers (myself included) go through as they move into a new identity—she was grieving for the more glamorous and independent parts of herself that she was temporarily disconnected from, and it really annoyed her to see them in anyone else, especially someone who she thought should be in the same boat she was. Alexis used that encounter to keep growing and developing herself—she didn't stop at her own initial emotional resistance, she pushed through and asked herself questions. She was introspective enough to recognize that her initial resistance to me had almost nothing to do with me but had everything to do with herself and where she needed to develop next. This little "hit" to her self-esteem was really an opportunity to learn more about herself. If you, like Alexis, can see your interactions with others—even the casual ones—as chances to get to know *yourself* better, you'll get a whole lot closer to the tremendous power of your bulletproof spirit.

It's All About You

The most important self-growth tends to come through the most personal and the most difficult hits we take in our relationships. When a bullet hits close to the bone, it can be hard to discipline ourselves to look for the personal growth. One big motivation for extracting the lessons we need from the most difficult of relationship hits is that lessons we don't learn may come back again and again in different forms until we have mastered them. Another motivation is that sometimes, the only good thing we can take away from these trials comes in the form of self-knowledge or personal growth—we can create meaning from our own suffering, heartache, or loss if we let the relationship be a teacher.

Consider Eileen, a woman in her late fifties whose husband had left her, married a much younger woman, and actually moved to Paris to "start over." The divorce had blindsided her. She was forced to move from a big house to a small apartment and had to work outside the home for the first time in more than thirty years. She was still very, very angry five years after the divorce and when she came to a workshop, she insisted that there wasn't one positive thing that had come from this devastating blow. With coaching, Eileen slowly began to acknowledge that, though she still didn't like her ex at all, she liked herself a whole lot more now than while she had been married. She was proud of her ability to take care of her own finances and she had overcome a lifelong fear of being alone. She admitted that for her entire adult life, she had been plagued by fears that she would end up alone. When her worst nightmare came true, she learned that she could survive and even thrive on her own. She came to see that these lessons gave her a kind of security that her marriage had never given her. She now recognizes how important the hit she took was to her own personal development. She's beginning to think it was worth the trade-off. Making it her business to extract every last drop of wisdom she can from the hit she took is empowering. While on the outside it might appear that she has taken a step backward, on the inside—where it really counts—she has come a very long way, indeed.

When you start to pay more attention to all of your "realationships," you will begin to see that your whole life has been a complex dance of love, loss, laughter, and tears and that you have been dancing with all the people you were meant to dance with. Like many of the secrets shared by spiritually bulletproof people, this one is most powerful if you can apply it in the unfolding *now*. When you start seeing every person you meet, know, love, or hate as a teacher placed in your path for an important reason, you will become infinitely closer to tapping into your full bulletproof potential.

• • •

Bounce Back Boot Camp

Here are some strategies for reevaluating and reframing your "realationships":

- Write a course description for a particular relationship where you've taken a hit. If you're not sure what a course description looks like, look online at a community college or adult education website and read a few course descriptions. It could start something like this: *Advanced Heartbreak Seminar: This nine-year intensive in love and loss will leave you prepared to find real and lasting love. Heavy assignment load. Will cover the following:*
  - *Handling betrayal*
  - *Forgiving the unforgivable*
  - *Learning to trust myself*

    Be creative and as specific as you can. Try to outline what your "realationship" offered as a course in the school of life. If you had seen the course description beforehand, would you have signed up? If not, what lessons would you have missed?
- Think about someone you feel a lot of resistance toward. Journal about your feelings of resentment. Try to uncover what it really is that pushes your buttons. What is it about *you* that your resistance might be signaling? For instance, one client found herself feeling resistant toward a friend who she felt was self-indulgent. This friend wouldn't skip a yoga class and she spent a lot of money on organic food for herself. She opted out of sitting on the annual fundraising committee at their kids' school because she felt she needed more downtime. Our client found herself thinking

that her friend was selfish for "putting herself first." We worked to uncover what it was about all this that really pushed her buttons. In the end, our client realized that she felt this resistance because she was resentful of all the pressures she felt in her life and she wasn't nurturing herself at all.

- If you've taken a serious hit in a particular relationship, especially if there's ongoing tension or you're estranged, put a photo of the person alone or with the two of you together somewhere you'll see it daily. Put a little note at the bottom of the photo that says: "This relationship is my teacher." Even if you don't believe this at first, just try it for a few weeks with as open a heart as you can muster. Every time you look at the picture, repeat to yourself, "This relationship is my teacher." See what bubbles up for you—you may be quite surprised.

● ● ●

Part Two

· · ·

A BULLETPROOF
BATTLE PLAN

SECRET #7

Entitlement Is the Enemy of Energy

Life is not a matter of holding good cards,
but of playing a poor hand well.

—ROBERT LOUIS STEVENSON

ONE OF THE MOST IMPORTANT SECRETS KNOWN TO SPIRITUALLY bulletproof people is that feelings of entitlement seriously sap the energy necessary to take any hit and come out on top. Spiritually fragile people spend a great deal of psychic, emotional, and physical energy reacting to the unfairness they're experiencing because they feel that they are *entitled* to a certain kind of life—one without hits that hurt. Spiritually resilient people resist these feelings of entitlement and use all of their energy and resources to do all they can with whatever it is they've been given. This one difference in attitude makes a tremendous difference in success and satisfaction and is well worth cultivating if you want to reap the full benefits of super spiritual resiliency.

The word *entitlement* refers to a person's right to receive a value or benefit of some kind. For instance, if you pay into the

Social Security system for thirty years, you are *entitled* to receive a retirement benefit from that system. The word itself generally refers to something guaranteed by law, but for our purposes here, let's think of entitlement as a personal belief or attitude. We live in a time and place that provides us with so much—we have material comforts, access to information and knowledge, medical care that can accomplish miracles, and more choices about lifestyle than ever before in history. Most of us have grown up in relative peace and prosperity and have come to expect more of the same. We have come to a point where we feel *entitled* to a certain kind of life—one that lives up to our highest standards. When we face adversity, it is especially easy to indulge a sense of entitlement because there is a very fine and slippery line between having high expectations for yourself and your life and believing that you have a *right* to a certain kind of life. While they certainly maintain high expectations in all areas of their lives, spiritually bulletproof people consciously resist feelings of entitlement and strive to gracefully play the hand they have been dealt.

> Spiritually bulletproof people consciously resist feelings of entitlement and strive to gracefully play the hand they've been dealt.

If you want to be spiritually bulletproof, you must become aware of your own feelings of entitlement and then commit yourself to taking responsibility for your situation exactly as it is. Most people never understand the tremendous power of this secret and spend their lives complaining about their situations and refusing to take total responsibility for working with whatever life presents. If you can train yourself away from your feelings of entitlement, you will be able to tap into the full power of your bulletproof spirit. In his famous essay "Self-Reliance," Ralph Waldo Emerson writes:

There is a time in every man's education when he arrives at the conviction that envy is ignorance; that imitation is suicide; that he must take himself for better, for worse, as his portion; that though the wide universe is full of good, no kernel of nourishing corn can come to him but through his toil bestowed on that plot of ground which is given him to till.

Every person on the planet is given a particular "plot of ground" to work with. This "plot of ground" is the entirety of who we are, the relationships we have, and the lives we are living. Without a doubt, some people seem to get much better plots! Some people seem to be *born* holding better real estate, and when we're in default mode, it is very easy to slip into feelings of envy, jealousy, and entitlement—all of which seriously undermine our ability to play the hand we've been dealt.

The "Right" Stuff

Let's take a look at some of the "rights" that we convince ourselves that we should have:

- We are entitled to have had an easy and happy childhood. We have the right to have been spared the stresses of divorce, familial conflict, or financial difficulties.
- We are entitled to look good and feel good at all times. We have a right to uninterrupted good health.
- We are entitled to be loved and respected by the other people in our lives. We have the right to be treated with care and attention.
- We are entitled to fulfilling and well-paid work that also allows us plenty of free time. We have the right to a successful career.
- We are entitled to financial comfort and a nice lifestyle. We have the right to security and pleasure.

- We are entitled to satisfying love relationships. We have the right to great sex and lots of romance.
- We are entitled to a smooth and trouble-free life. We have the right to an anxiety- and stress-free daily existence.

Now, you might be thinking "Of course I am entitled to these things! Are you telling me I shouldn't want all of this?" We would never tell you not to want or go after all of these things—it's only normal to want them and *we* definitely do! It is very important to have high expectations for yourself and your life because your thoughts, desires, and intentions help build your life. But there is a huge difference between having high expectations and having a sense of entitlement. Having high expectations sends a powerful and positive signal to others and out into the universe, helping to attract whatever will serve the highest good in your life. But having an attitude of entitlement sends a powerful negative signal to others and out into the universe, limiting your ability to create the life you want because all of your energy is going toward resenting the fact that you're not getting what you think you deserve.

Strong Medicine

Becoming aware of and eradicating a sense of entitlement requires strength, humility, and maturity. We've seen through our personal and professional experience how threatening it can be to change in this area. When our sense of entitlement is challenged, we can become defensive and angry because we think we're being asked to give up something that we need. Please be assured that when you move away from your own sense of entitlement, you will find a whole new way of perceiving yourself and your life that will be much more empowering.

You may feel entitled to something that you think would have been better for you than what you actually received. For example, maybe you believe that you were entitled to a childhood that was happier or healthier than the one you experienced. You may have spent years and even decades of your adult life resenting your parents and upbringing and being haunted by painful memories, insecurities, and fears that you developed as a result of what you lived through. Maybe your adult relationships are affected by what happened when you were a kid. As someone who has done extensive work on healing from and forgiving aspects of my own upbringing, I have a lot of compassion for other people who feel this way about their own childhoods. I truly understand the way that losses during childhood have a profound impact on adult life and leave holes in your heart so big you think that nothing will ever be able to fill them.

What we are asking from you right now is that you open your heart and mind to some new ways of thinking about your past that will help you much, much more than holding on to your seething resentments ever will. Carrying around the pain of the past is like trying to live your life with a 75-pound bag of cement on your back. If you really want to put that weight down once and for all and experience how light and free life can be, you must begin to look at things in a whole new way—a way that might seem challenging at first.

There are some very important chapters on forgiveness coming up, and they will give you some powerful new tools to get free from the pain of your past. For now, please try to keep your mind and heart open. Letting go of a sense of entitlement is not about condoning wrong behavior or letting your parents or anyone else "off the hook." Eradicating your sense of entitlement is about letting *yourself,* and your *heart,* off a hook that has been really hurting you for a long time. It's about learning to see in a new way—one that will bring peace to your heart and replace the pain and anxiety that feelings of entitlement exacerbate. Understand that your feelings of entitlement do not protect or help you in any way—all they do is make you continually unhappy and sap the energy you need to bounce back from these blows. They cause you to keep suffering long after the people or things that hurt you are out of the picture. Letting go of your own feelings of entitlement is not saying that what other people did was okay and it is not saying that there should be no consequences for their behavior. All we're really suggesting is that you choose to let go of a kind of mental torture that you put yourself through. Pay attention to how you feel when you read about Michael's story about his own struggles with feelings of entitlement:

> For many years of my adult life I could not get past feeling that I had somehow been deprived of some of my rights to a happy, carefree childhood, and it seemed obvious to me that many of the struggles I faced in my grown-up life were directly or indirectly connected to being deprived of these rights. I went to therapy, prayed a lot, meditated, and read all kinds of books on forgiveness. No matter how much my mind analyzed and no matter how much I examined things, I could never really let go of the anger, emptiness, and sense of loss I felt about certain parts of my past. I felt that I had been deprived of something that I deserved. One day I was at a workshop where I learned the Native American tradition of setting my stones in the medicine wheel. The wise old woman who was teaching the ritual talked to us about our parents, grandparents, and ancestors and showed us how to set their stones in the wheel. She talked to us about the importance of honoring these people. One of the other participants asked a question that I'm sure many in the room wanted to ask—what if you don't feel like honoring your parents? What if they did things that were not honorable? This wise teacher responded in a way that I never expected and that changed me forever. She gave us a stern but grandmotherly lecture about the ignorance of our expectations and the ingratitude and lack of wisdom in our sense of entitlement. She asked some basic questions about our pasts: Had our parents brought us into the world and helped give us the bodies we were living in? Had we been fed? Were we clothed and sheltered? Were we given opportunities to get an education? We all nodded affirmatively to

her questions and watched as she shook her head at us. She re-
minded us of the precious gift of life itself given to us by our
parents. She pointed out the many qualities, talents, and char-
acteristics our parents had given us as our genetic inheritance.
She made clear her sense that to expect more than these abun-
dant gifts was to indulge inappropriate feelings of entitlement.
What right had we to question all we had been given and de-
cide that it was inadequate? She compared our situations with
those of most of the inhabitants on the earth and throughout his-
tory, and she asked us how we dared ask for more than we had
been given. I felt something soften inside me as I let her wisdom
sink in. I began to humble myself just enough to question my
own sense of entitlement.

Make a point right now to notice how you felt as you read
Michael's story. Did you feel anger seeping up through the
cracks? Did you feel resistance to any of his statements? If you experienced negative feelings when contemplating these ideas
about eradicating entitlement, that is perfectly normal. You have
probably been holding so much pain for so long that your unconscious mind rebels at the idea of letting it go. Eradicating a
sense of entitlement, like forgiving the people and situations that
have hurt you, seems, at first, like asking you to give something
up that you deserve to hold on to or that in some way serves
you. Nothing could be further from the truth! If you keep going
now—if you push through this initial resistance and keep reading the upcoming chapters and try the techniques they suggest—
you will begin to see that you can use these secrets to free
yourself from the pain of your past and bounce back completely
from even the worst hits. These techniques have worked for us
personally and for thousands and thousands of people, and they
will work for you. Try a new way and see the results for yourself.

Start opening up to the possibility that your life up till this
point has been perfectly preparing you for all you're meant to do

with the rest of your life. You may never have willingly chosen the things or situations that hurt you, but maybe they have served the evolution of your spirit in some profound way that you cannot yet understand but that will be revealed as your destiny unfolds. Spiritually bulletproof people understand that they don't know everything and that they don't even always understand what's in their own best interests. Though they may grieve for the childhoods or other things or experiences they never had, they understand on a very deep level that they were not *entitled* to have anything they didn't have. Resilient people don't squander their energy resenting what they weren't given or didn't have—they reserve their energy for gracefully playing whatever hands they've been dealt. Spiritually bulletproof people dwell as much as they can in gratitude for whatever is and they commit themselves to working with what they've got. They know that someone else's "plot of ground" might have better soil and fewer rocks, but they don't waste themselves thinking thoughts like "I deserved a better lot in life." They trust that the plot they've been given to till is the right one for them in some way that they may not even understand. They commit themselves to cultivating beautiful gardens no matter how poor the land they've been given to work. While spiritually fragile people waste their precious energy complaining about the unfairness of life, their resilient counterparts are already watching the fruits of their labors begin to bloom.

Entitlement Is an Extension of the Ego

Feelings of entitlement spring in part from a false assumption about our own ability to know what is best for us or what serves the highest good. A sense of entitlement reveals the erroneous belief that we would not take any heartbreaking hits if we had the life we deserved. Spiritually fragile people have a strong sense that they know what is best and how things should be. Their egos tell them that they are entitled to different things and more than they got or are getting. Spiritually bulletproof people accept that everything about their past, their present, and their "plot of ground" is exactly as it had to be and should be. Spiritually bulletproof people are uncompromising in this belief; they know that it makes no sense to believe that some parts of the past were meant to be while others should never have happened. Albert Einstein once said "Either nothing is a miracle, or everything is," and resilient people understand that they can't have it both ways—either none of the past makes sense or all of it does. This belief helps them resist feelings of entitlement because they know, deep down, that they got and are getting exactly what they need for their lessons this time around. They resist their own sense of entitlement because they see how it steals their energy away from the real work at hand—playing the cards they've been dealt with courage, good will, faith, and gratitude. They know an important secret: Every hand is a winning hand when it's held by a person willing to play it for all it's worth.

• • •

Bounce Back Boot Camp

Try these ideas for fine-tuning your expectations and eradicating your sense of entitlement:

- One of the best ways to begin to loosen the grip of feelings of entitlement—especially related to your childhood—is to consciously choose to focus on gratitude for what you did and do have. Try this simple, abbreviated version of "setting your stones in the wheel" and see what happens:
  - *You'll need to collect some small stones for this ceremony. Choose one for yourself and one for each person in your family. Try to find stones that symbolize each individual; for example, you may choose certain sizes or colors that strike you as being appropriate for each person.*
  - *Keep the stones in a small bag or bowl on your nightstand and*

each evening before you go to sleep, place the stones in your "wheel." Place your stone in the center and spend a few moments reflecting on something you're grateful for about yourself or your life.

- *Next, place the stones of your family members, one at a time, around your stone, pausing each time to reflect upon one thing that you're grateful for having received from each person.*
- *It may be difficult for you to find something that you feel grateful for but find some little thing to focus on, even if it is just a physical trait you inherited. Think about your physical traits, your talents, and natural strengths, the qualities your own children may have inherited—anything that you can find to appreciate.*
- *Try to find new things to be grateful for each time you set the stones, but if you are struggling, it's okay to focus on the same things over and over. As you set a stone, say something like "I am grateful for my healthy, shiny hair, which I inherited from my mother" or "I am grateful to my dad for passing on his love of music to me."*
- *In certain cases, you might find it almost impossible to find something for which to be grateful. Try saying something like "I am grateful to my mother for giving me the gift of life." If negative thoughts, memories, or feelings pop up as you are setting the stones, practice thought-stopping and stay focused on gratitude.*
- The healing power of this simple ceremony is cumulative—you must do it every day for at least a week, preferably a month. We've had many clients over the years tell us that this activity helped them break through blocks that they couldn't surmount in all their years of talking about or rehashing their childhood wounds.
- Cut up some small slips of paper. On each slip, write down something you felt or feel entitled to. Maybe you feel entitled to parents who unconditionally support you or to not having any financial worries. Try to be honest with

yourself—it's okay to have feelings of entitlement that you have to release. Be as exhaustive as you can—try to write down anything you feel that you somehow "deserve." Now, read through your slips and consider the energy you have given or continue to give to these feelings of entitlement. Safely burn all the slips and watch as the smoke from the fire disappears up the chimney or out into the air. Feel yourself releasing these feelings of entitlement and acknowledge that you're freeing up your energy to better assist you in living your best life now.

- Buy a small cactus or perhaps some stalks of bamboo. Choose a plant that is very hardy in less-than-ideal conditions. (I've had three stalks of bamboo that I've totally neglected for the last three years and they are growing and thriving. I just change the water in the vase every month or so.) Set your plant where you see it daily and observe its ability to thrive. Know that you are no hothouse orchid— like your plant, you can thrive in any conditions.

●　●　●

Grieve Like a Guru

Healing is a matter of time,
but sometimes also a matter of opportunity.

—HIPPOCRATES

IF YOU WANT TO BE ABLE TO TAKE ANY HIT AND COME OUT ON TOP, it's essential that you master the art of grieving. Spiritually bulletproof people are very good at doing something that most people in our culture try to avoid like the plague—they know how important it is to grieve when they have taken a heartbreaking hit. Spiritually fragile people underestimate the importance of the grieving process or they grieve in ways that don't facilitate true and lasting healing and recovery. The ability to bounce back after taking a bullet often hinges on being able to mourn in a highly effective way. Since we live in a culture that is completely out of touch with and in denial about grief, you may have to develop new ideas about and new strategies for grieving in a way that will turbo-charge your resiliency. The good news is that you can learn to grieve like a guru and help yourself to handle any hit that comes your way.

You may not realize how very anti-grief we are in our modern Western world. Our society encourages us to repress our feelings of grief and to move quickly past any grief we do feel. Grief is a natural and necessary part of life, but we have lost sight of its necessity and its benefits. And the grieving process is much more than just a necessary evil that we have to deal with—it's actually one of the most valuable and transformative experiences we can go through. There is an old Turkish proverb that says "He that conceals his grief finds no remedy for it." When we deny ourselves proper grieving, we deprive ourselves of a necessary step in bouncing back after a blow. While no one looks forward to having to grieve, spiritually bulletproof people honor their grief by making time and space to mourn fully and deeply.

> Spiritually bulletproof people honor their grief by making time and space to mourn fully and deeply.

Grief is not just an emotion—it is a process. The grieving process takes up time and uses up space in our minds, hearts, relationships, and lives. Often, we do not give ourselves permission to take up time and space for something that we consider sad and depressing and that others make us feel is self-indulgent or immature. It's really important to realize that this response to grief is a very modern phenomenon, and it's not a positive development or sign of progress. A devaluing of the grieving or mourning process is a mental, emotional, and spiritual regression within our culture that we must reverse in our own lives if we want to tap into our bulletproof potential.

When Things Went Bad in the Good Old Days

In our age of medical miracles and wonder drugs, we live without the specter of death hanging over us every day. But one hundred years ago, things were much different. Disease, lack of sterile practices, poor nutrition, and rudimentary medical care made early death much more prevalent. It was so common for women to die in childbirth that many women made arrangements for the care of their infant in the event that they did not survive delivery. Antibiotics hadn't been discovered and people routinely died from things as simple as small cuts. Couples had large families because infectious diseases such as typhoid, whooping cough, and tuberculosis claimed the lives of many children, and they hoped to have at least a few offspring survive. In underdeveloped and developing nations, not much has changed. In times and places where people have less control over death, mourning and grieving customs and rituals tend to be clearly defined and adhered to. Grieving was (and is still, in some parts of the world) a large part of the average person's life; mourning was often done in formalized stages and with the support of the larger community. It was often quite extended, lasting for months or years. There were practices and routines in place for someone who was grieving, and these prescribed actions helped facilitate healing and recovery from loss.

Obviously, no one wants to go back to these "good old days," and working to eradicate these conditions in underdeveloped nations should be a global priority. We have so much to be grateful for here in the modern world—we have so much more control over pain, suffering, and death itself. But we've thrown the baby out with the bathwater—while it's a blessing that we have fewer early deaths to grieve, we have also lost our connection with the rituals and customs that help us grieve when we need to. No advances of science or medicine can make grief obsolete. To be human is to sustain losses. We still lose loved ones and get ill ourselves. And there are the other losses that take their toll—financial fiascoes, marital meltdowns, and career crises. When we take these hits now, we have no idea how to mourn and grieve and, therefore, we have no idea how to feel better. Most of us have lost contact with the cultural and religious rituals and practices that support grieving, and the ones that do survive often leave us feeling like we're just going through the motions. If you've taken a serious hit, you need to seriously grieve. But it's hard to grieve when you have never learned how to and when no one around you is encouraging it. If you want super spiritual resiliency, learn how to grieve and then do it like you mean it.

A Permission Slip

We live in a speeded-up culture that wants us to do everything really fast. We want dinner on the table in fifteen minutes and our facelifts over a long weekend. This fast-track mentality extends to the heartbreaking hits we take, as well. Even death is expected to obey the hyperscheduled pace we've established. Three days are allowed for wakes, viewings, and funerals, and then about a week later, everyone involved is expected to "get back to normal." If a widower is still crying or isolating himself one month after the loss of his wife, people begin to hint that he really needs to "get on with his life." We've worked with many people who have felt tremendous pressure to "get back to normal" after taking serious losses. While there's usually an onslaught of support in the early days of a loss or death, it is rare for grieving to be encouraged for any extended period. It's really important for you to give yourself permission to resist this pressure to compress, repress, or expedite your grief. We want you to think of this chapter as a kind of permission slip. Since no one is going to give you permission to grieve with gusto, we want you to consider this your official go-ahead to mourn with all your might. You can tell everybody that "the experts" (we did write the book, after all!) say that you must go through a very serious grieving period. You don't need to feel guilty or self-indulgent for deciding to grieve—it is the wisest thing you can do. Plus, we're making you do it—so blame us and join the ranks of the spiritually bulletproof.

Take It Like a Man (or Woman!)

Shakespeare's *Macbeth* is one of the bloodiest plays in the English language—lots of hits taken all around. In one scene, a nobleman named Macduff returns home to find that Macbeth has murdered his wife and all of his children. His comrades urge him to react "like a man" to this heartbreaking hit. Macduff tells them, "I will answer it like a man, but first I must feel it like a man." This line shows Macduff's true strength—he is strong enough to allow himself to experience the depth of his anguish. It is very common for people who have taken serious hits to suffer doubly—they grieve for the loss they've experienced and then they feel guilty or weak because they're grieving! To really experience the depths of your own despair is the bravest and most powerful thing you can do when faced with a hit. To grieve intensely is the truest way to "take it like a man" (or woman). Spiritually bulletproof people realize that society's take on grieving is seriously askew and they don't feel guilty, weak, or immature for mourning like they mean it. There's a Hindu saying that translates roughly as "Don't leave the road until the road leaves you," and, in this vein, resilient people do not leave their grieving until their grieving leaves them.

Sometimes, people's ideas about spirituality actually get in the way of their grieving process. Sara came to a workshop and told us that she felt like all her years of practicing Buddhist meditation should have prepared her to take the loss of her twenty-two-year marriage with greater calm and acceptance. She confessed that she was ashamed at her lack of equanimity, or tranquility and composure, in the face of her heartbreak. She believed that she must not have made much spiritual progress if she felt as grief-stricken as she did. Sara's feelings are quite common; we have noticed that many people think that being "spiritual" means that you won't need to grieve as much as the average person. And there *are* some very enlightened individuals who genuinely do handle all that comes their way with great equanimity. But when Macduff tells his men that he will "answer it like a man" only after "feeling it like a man," he is on target about the proper order of things. Intense and protracted grief and equanimity are not mutually exclusive. In fact, the process of grieving itself can be a stepping-stone on the path to balance. In the end, Sara was able to see that she needed to allow herself time and space to mourn the loss of her marriage and needed to stop judging herself as less than spiritually evolved because she couldn't transcend her pain on demand. Our spirits *are* bulletproof, but our hearts, minds, and bodies are only human—grieving like a human is part of the spiritual journey, not a spiritual failure.

The Riches of Ritual

One of the ways that spiritually bulletproof people maximize the effectiveness of their grieving process is by engaging in ritual. The word *ritual* means different things to different people, but for our purposes, think of it as referring to an intentional and defined period of mourning. The Jewish tradition of sitting shiva is a good example of a grieving ritual that is still practiced to great effect by many people. Jews bury their dead as soon as possible as a way of showing respect, but they then spend seven days after the funeral sitting shiva in the home of the mourners. Extended family, friends, and members of the community converge at the home and bring prayers, condolences, and food. During this weeklong ritual, all normal daily routines are prohibited— all energy is focused on grieving so that healing may begin and so that those mourning will be able to better reenter normal life at the end of the week. All the mirrors in the home are covered so that mourners can look like hell if they feel like it and not be reminded of their disheveled appearance. Those grieving do not prepare any food—family and friends arrange everything so that all energy stays on mourning the loss. The Jewish tradition encourages active and intense mourning and discourages any efforts to "cheer up" those grieving. Sitting shiva is one religious tradition that is also a cultural tradition among nonreligious Jews. There are also many other religious and cultural traditions that offer great comfort when people have taken heartbreaking hits. When Azim's son was killed, the ritual of his Ismaili Muslim faith called for a grieving period of forty days during which the entire community supports those mourning with prayer, food, and companionship. This ritualized period of mourning was one of the most important factors in Azim's ability to survive the loss of his only son. The rituals of our cultural and religious heritage can also serve as a place to start when creating new and personalized rituals for grieving. Sometimes there aren't any rituals that we can look toward to help us through a loss—we must create our own. When I lost my baby six months along into a normal pregnancy, there was no sitting shiva or other religious tradition to help me process my grief. I decided that very first day that I was going to grieve intentionally and intensely so that I could recover and go on with my life. I decided that I wouldn't leave my house for three weeks. I also gave myself permission to stay in bed for the entire time if I wanted to. I allowed my family and friends to cook for me and gave myself permission to not even try to feel better or okay. After the first week, I started renting tearjerker movies just to keep myself crying as much as possible. I intuitively sensed that, for me, three weeks was what I probably needed, but I also wasn't planning to be rigid about it because, in many cases, grieving may be much more protracted than this and I wanted to allow myself enough time to mourn fully. Sure enough, at the end of the three weeks, I stopped mourning. I still had sad days, but, like Macduff, I had "felt it like a man" and I was ready to live again.

The next few chapters focus on different aspects of grieving, but the first step you must take in order to grieve like a guru is to get intentional about mourning what you've lost. Whether you've lost a beloved family member, a marriage, a breast, a job, a friendship, or a dream—give yourself the gift of feeling your grief as deeply and for as long as you need to. When Rumi, the thirteenth-century Sufi mystic and poet, tells us "The cure for pain is in the pain," he is reaching across the centuries to remind us of the ancient wisdom of giving ourselves fully to our grief so that we may return fully to the happy lives that wait beyond our pain.

* * *

Bounce Back Boot Camp

Get in touch with your inner "grief guru" by trying out these ideas:

- Educate yourself about grief and the grieving process. Knowledge really *is* power, and when you're trying to come out on top of a hit, you need as much power as you can get. Go online and research or ask your librarian or bookseller about books about grieving. Rabbi Harold Kushner's *When Bad Things Happen to Good People* is a must-read. Elisabeth Kübler-Ross's *On Death and Dying* is a classic that will demystify the process of grieving. Know that when you grieve, you are not alone—you are connected to all of the great souls who have ever lived and died.
- Someone doesn't have to die for you to get in touch with your grief. It is important to grieve for all different types of hits, large and small. Do not dismiss your own sadness and pain as being unjustified—all loss must be honored. For example, many people don't allow themselves to really grieve "invisible losses" like very early miscarriages. Using your journal, make a list of what you might tell yourself are "little losses," and as you write, notice your feelings. Do any of these losses seem to call to you, asking you to grieve them? If so, plan a ritual to do so.
- When you are grieving, give yourself the gift of loving self-care. Part of the ritual of grieving may involve taking special care of yourself, body, mind, and soul. If you've taken

a hit and need to grieve your loss, make the decision to nurture yourself during this particular period of time. Treat yourself like you would a sick child—feed yourself comforting food, surround yourself with softness and love, and don't push yourself to do much. Grieving is the time to take it easy and be very gentle with yourself.

• • •

Spend Forty Days in the Fire

*A great grief has taught
me more than any minister.*

—LOUISA MAY ALCOTT

SPIRITUALLY FRAGILE PEOPLE SEE SUFFERING AS AN ENEMY AND THEY experience times of grief or depression as meaningless and useless periods of stagnation. Spiritually bulletproof people understand that, without exception, periods of trial and suffering are also times of profound transformation and growth. They use these times "in the fire" as opportunities for spiritual refinement, and this mindset strengthens and sustains them when the going gets tough.

The English poet William Cowper believed that "Grief is itself a medicine" and spiritually resilient people are aware of the "medicinal" properties of the suffering they endure as a result of the bullets that come their way. While no one looks forward to feeling grief, pain, or depression, spiritually bulletproof people believe that time spent "in the fire" fuels their spiritual progress.

This ability to find value in their suffering gives spiritually resilient people a real edge in life. You can give yourself a tremendous boost in resiliency if you are willing to see your times of trial as opportunities to turbo-charge your spiritual progress.

> Spiritually bulletproof people believe that time spent "in the fire" fuels their spiritual progress.

A Double Feature

Whether or not you realize it consciously, you are really living two lives simultaneously. One is the material existence that is visible to the world and the other is the inner life of your spirit—a private existence invisible to all but you. You may not have ever thought about yourself and your life in this way before, but try to expand your sense of yourself to include both of these identities. It's almost as if there are two movies running simultaneously in adjacent theaters—two different stories are unfolding at the same time and they are both about you! On one screen is the course of events and the cast of characters that make up the story line of your "real life." It is a plot-driven film—lots of action. On the other screen is the story of your spirit's evolution. This film captures your inner journey—it shows how far you've come as a spiritual being. Your growth in patience, faith, and love is documented, as is every development of your spirit. Now, most people focus all their attention on the plot-driven movie because there's so much going on and it looks very exciting. Spiritually resilient people know that the real action is happening in the theater next door! If you want to take any hit and come out on top, realize that you really have a kind of double identity. Your outer life and your inner life are unfolding side by side, and sometimes when the worst stuff is happening on the screen in theater 1, the very best stuff is going on in theater 2 next door. Spiritually bulletproof people believe that success in their inner lives is possible even when things have gone to hell in a handbasket in their outer lives. They know a powerful secret: The worst pain and suffering they experience in their real-world journeys can fuel their greatest progress on their inner journeys.

If you can begin to give greater weight to your inner life, you will start to see the suffering and pain you experience in your outer life differently. It will no longer define you the way it once did, because you will develop an expanded sense of your own identity. If you take a minute to think about people like physicist Stephen Hawking or the late actor Christopher Reeve, it is easy to see that a person's physical or material life may become extremely limited, and yet, at the same time, the inner life may expand exponentially. Think about someone like Nelson Mandela, whose outer life was completely circumscribed by his twenty-seven years in prison but whose inner life flourished magnificently. These heroic figures show us what is possible when we understand that our inner lives are even more valuable than our outer ones.

Getting Fired

Think about a potter making a vase on his wheel. He shapes and smooths the clay into the desired shape and then paints on a glaze. At this point, the vase is not all it must become—it is still just soft clay that is fragile, useless, and dull. It must be subjected to the intense fires of the kiln for it to become strong, useful, and lustrous. Its time in the fire is what transforms the clay into a work of art and a fully functional object. It is the time in the fire that creates the real magic. And this is as true for us as it is for the vase—we may be formed and full of potential but it is only through our "times in the fire" that we are made strong and shining. When the hits we take plunge us into the fires of pain and anguish, we must try to remember that we are being transformed into beings of greater strength, usefulness, and beauty.

This chapter is called "Spend Forty Days in the Fire" because it is necessary for spiritually bulletproof people to be intentional about the process of both grieving and spiritual refinement. If you have taken a serious or devastating hit, you might need to spend an extended period in the fire of mourning and transformation. We use the example of forty days in the fire because forty is a powerful number for ritual and transformation. Moses spent forty days on Mount Sinai, Jesus spent forty days in the desert, and Muslims grieve their dead for forty days. Lent lasts for forty days, and the rains fell on Noah for forty days and nights. If you spend forty days in the fire, you can bet good money that you'll come out transformed.

Labor Pains

The metaphor of being "in the fire" is an apt one for people who are grieving. It's hard to imagine greater suffering than being burned by fire. I knew of a man who was burned over a large percentage of his body and whose pain was indescribable. This man was a former Marine and very tough and brave, but his pain was so intense that he repeatedly begged his best friend to kill him and put him out of his misery. The friend would not agree to help him, and he endured two years of terrible suffering through skin grafts and other operations. In the end, he was deeply grateful to his friend for refusing his request and he was very happy to be alive even though he was quite disfigured.

When you've taken a devastating hit, the pain and anguish can make you feel as though you're literally in the fire. It can feel unbearable. You may feel as though you cannot take it anymore and that it will never end. Being in the fire can feel like hell on Earth, and it's only natural to want to escape from it any way you can. But it's really important to remember that the only real way out of the fire is by going through it. It can be enormously helpful if you are able to think of the pain of the fire as being transformative. If you can hold on to the truth that the fire is refining your spirit, you will find the grief and agony you're feeling to be more bearable.

Spiritually bulletproof people understand that these periods of trial and suffering we all must go through have redemptive value. Think about what a woman goes through when she is in labor. Anyone who has ever had a baby will tell you that, though it is the most amazing experience to be had in life, it is no walk in the park. During the transition phase of labor, it is very common for women to feel as though they may die from their pain. How amazing it is that most women go on to have more babies! But the pain of labor makes sense to us because it has a clear purpose that makes it all worthwhile. It is extremely helpful during labor to focus on the prize of the healthy baby who waits at the end of the labor. The pain of each contraction is balanced by the knowledge that each contraction brings progress toward birth. Just as the pain of labor brings new life into the world, the pain of being in the fire helps us give birth to our finer and stronger selves.

Fire-Walking

Spiritually resilient people resist the urge to repress or minimize their own intense grief or pain. They stay in the fire for as long as it takes to burn itself out and they are helped along by their knowledge that their pain is fueling their own spiritual evolution. If you want to tap into your bulletproof potential, use your time in the fire to grieve as intensely as you can. Push into rather than away from the pain. Rather than running away, walk further into the fire so that you can come out on the other side ready to live again.

• • •

Bounce Back Boot Camp

Here are some ways to walk further into the fire:

- Make a conscious decision to walk through the fire of your grief or pain for as long as it takes to burn itself out. Commit ahead of time.

- Tell the people in your life that you will be devoting yourself to working through your anguish or loss for a particular time period. Let them know that you need to cut back on other commitments so that you can focus on being in the fire.

- Do not try to have a positive attitude, look at the bright side, or in any way minimize or avoid the depth of your pain. This is your time to indulge your pain and all negative feelings as fully as you can.

- Spend time looking through photos or correspondence connected to the loss you've taken. Listen to music that reminds you of the person involved or that gets you feeling emotional. Use your senses to help you stay in touch with your feelings.

- Talk about your grief or pain as much or as little as you want. Withdraw into yourself if that's what you feel like doing. Don't answer your phone, e-mails, or invitations. On the other hand, if you want to vent, reminisce, or just babble about your loss or suffering, feel free to impose on your family and friends as much as you need to during this time you've marked for being in the fire.

- Watch sad movies. Sometimes it is hard to cry even when you want to. Crying is an excellent physical and psychological release, so try to do it a lot during this time.

- Write in your journal. Keep your notebook near you and try to express yourself as much as you can. Record memories, resentments, fears that arise, feelings of despair, things you'd like to say to others, anything that arises. Even if you don't feel like writing, make yourself do it a couple of times a week—it's very cathartic in ways that surprise most "nonwriters."

- Pray or meditate. Ask for divine support during your time in the fire. Pray for strength to walk deep into the fire through your most difficult feelings.

- Remember the Hindu expression "Don't leave the road

until the road leaves you." It's important to stay in the fire until the fire is out of you. Let yourself be sick and tired until you're sick and tired of being sick and tired! Make yourself miserable until you're miserable being miserable. Basically, get it out of your system by grieving until you can't grieve anymore. Let your time line emerge from the inside out.

• • •

SECRET #10

Avoid Anesthesia

*Numbing the pain for a while
will make it worse when you finally feel it.*

—ALBUS DUMBLEDORE
(from *Harry Potter and the Goblet of Fire* by J. K. Rowling)

THE ONLY WAY TO COME OUT ON TOP OF A HEARTBREAKING HIT IS to actually deal with it and be done with it, and there's no way to be done with it if you've avoided doing the difficult work of completely grieving your loss. Since spiritually bulletproof people understand that the antidote for their pain can be found somewhere inside their pain, they allow themselves to feel the depths of it and discipline themselves to push *into* it rather than *away* from it. Spiritually fragile people often try to avoid the terrible discomfort that their hits inflict by anesthetizing themselves in any number of ways. While they may buy themselves some temporary relief, it is this very behavior that prevents them from truly rebounding like their more resilient counterparts. If you want to bounce back from the bullet you've taken, it's vital that you make healthy and empowering choices at this critical juncture in your life—you must resist the urge to escape from your pain or numb yourself, even though it is natural to want to do just that.

Playwright and Nobel Prize winner George Bernard Shaw tells us that "Alcohol is the anesthesia by which we endure the operation of life," and for many people, he is absolutely right. There are also many other forms of anesthesia that people rely on to get through the tough stuff, and most of us have tried at least a few of them. While there's noth-

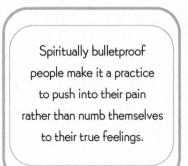

Spiritually bulletproof people make it a practice to push into their pain rather than numb themselves to their true feelings.

ing wrong with alleviating anxiety with an occasional drink, spiritually bulletproof people make it a practice to push into their pain rather than numb themselves to their true feelings.

This chapter is absolutely *not* about you giving up the things that give you pleasure in life—but it *is* about making sure that you make choices and engage in behaviors that turbo-charge your ability to bounce back after taking a hit. There is a fine line between doing things to relax or forget your troubles a little bit and getting into habits that end up anesthetizing you at a time when this can really prevent you from recovering from your loss. We want you to know that we have been there, just like you have, hurting really badly and just wanting it all to go away. We understand the desire to just be numb or completely escape from the pain or pressure you're experiencing. You are not alone—we are here to help you take care of yourself during this time of crisis or grief, and you truly can do things for yourself that will be far better than anesthetizing yourself from the pain. If you avoid anesthesia now, you will begin to tap into your own reserves of resiliency and be much closer to the finish line of this ordeal.

Cry Once

Have you ever done any remodeling at your house? Anyone who has ever endured this special brand of hell knows that it is a prolonged and expensive stress-fest that has been known to break up marriages! The last time we went through the remodeling ordeal at my house, we debated doing the project in stages that would allow us to keep more of the house in a normal state but would take much longer to finish. I'm really grateful that I listened to my husband's advice: He thought it would be better to "cry once" than to drag it out over a longer period of time. It's kind of like taking a bandage off—it's gonna hurt either way, so just rip that baby off! Getting through anything difficult usually involves hard work and some type of suffering—most of the time, getting it over with is the best choice even though it can be pretty tempting to do anything for a little relief. When you've taken a heartbreaking blow and you're "in the fire" of grief or mourning, your best course of action is usually to "cry once" and avoid anything that will prolong your ordeal. The sooner you fully and deeply grieve, the sooner you'll get to the happiness that really does wait on the other side of the hit you've taken.

Martinis, Macchiatos, Meds, and More . . .

We live in a culture that convinces us that pain, anguish, exhaustion, and depression are feelings to be avoided and eliminated as much as possible. Take a look at some of the everyday ways that we anesthetize ourselves from "negative" feelings:

- If we are exhausted, we dose up on caffeine rather than stopping and resting.
- If we are stressed out after a rotten day at a job we wish we could quit, we have a few beers to "take the edge off" rather than honor our desire to find work that we enjoy.
- If we are lonely, we go shopping even though we don't

have the money and what would really fill us up is a human connection.

- If we're bored, we zone out in front of the television or play video games rather than find out what really fulfills us.
- If we feel anxious, we start eating to temporarily stuff down our uneasiness.
- If we're in an unhappy relationship, we work all the time so we don't have to face realities at home.

It's important to note that sometimes it's okay to just escape from or avoid feelings in the very short term. A little denial can be a very useful strategy in certain situations. But when you have taken a serious hit and are trying to come out on top of it, your overall game plan must include a full-on face-off with your feelings, no matter how much you'd like to avoid them. The transcendental philosopher Ralph Waldo Emerson believed that "Society everywhere is in conspiracy against the manhood of every one of its members," and it is definitely true that we live in a society and culture that make us more likely to reject and run from any of our more difficult feelings. And it is this very avoidance that prevents us from tapping into the spiritual resiliency we so desperately need to handle the hits that come our way.

Maybe you have bought into the misguided belief that "negative" feelings are unnecessary and even damaging. A great deal can be said about the power of positive thinking, but rejecting your negative emotions is often a missed opportunity. Your feelings are like a rainbow—they comprise a full spectrum of mental and emotional states, from pure joy through deepest despair. When you judge the "darker" feelings like anger, sadness, and fear as being "bad" and to be avoided at all costs, it's as if you're only appreciating half of the colors of the rainbow. Contrary to the messages we get from advertising and the media, so-called "negative" feeling states are a necessary and beneficial part of the human experience. Clearly, depression or anxiety that is not related to an event or other life trigger and that persists over time needs to be addressed with a professional who may prescribe medication. But when the difficult feelings you're dealing with arise as a result of a serious hit you've taken, they are perfectly normal and should be allowed to work themselves out over time. Sadly, in our culture of quick fixes, these normal feelings of pain and sadness get pathologized—it seems that nowadays, when the going gets tough, the tough get medication.

You Are a Microcosm

While there are certainly cases where medication is a godsend, way too many of us are being convinced that there's something wrong with us when we are really just experiencing the normal and healthy suffering that comes from being "in the fire." If you look to nature as a model, you will see how normal and natural it is for things to fluctuate and go to extremes. The laws that affect the natural world also work upon the people who inhabit it—you are a little piece of the universe, cut from the same cloth of creation. What's true for the macrocosm is also true for the microcosm. Think about the variation in temperature from sweltering summer to bitterest winter. Think about the sea in its extremes of tranquility and tempest. Think about how the rain and the sun dance their duet for us and make life interesting, not to mention make everything grow. Why should you be any different from the natural world that is the macrocosm to your microcosm? Would you want a world with no rain, no wind, no snow, no storms? Do you really want a life without all of its emotions, even the more challenging ones? A lot of times, it is self-doubt that makes us scared of our own feelings—self-doubt that comes from living in a culture that makes these natural feelings out to be some kind of problem that must be eradicated. When you've read enough magazine ads and seen enough television commercials touting the benefits of the latest antidepressants, anti-anxiety medications, and sleeping pills, it's all too easy to think that there's something wrong with you if you have any sad or anxious feelings at all or if you're not sleeping well. Let's get real—if you've taken a heartbreaking or otherwise serious blow, there'd be something wrong with you if you *didn't* feel awful. You've probably seen those little quizzes they put in the ads for certain medications, the ones with questions like "Have you lost interest in activities that you used to enjoy?" or "Are you having trouble sleeping?" and maybe they've made you wonder if you need medication. Only you and your doctor can make these decisions, but we can tell you that if you've taken a bullet recently or haven't fully dealt with one from the past, then *of course* you've lost interest in activities you used to enjoy and *of course* you're having trouble sleeping. Maybe the answer isn't that you should anesthetize yourself to these feelings. Maybe the answer is that you should work your way through them, knowing that feeling bad is normal and natural when something bad has happened to you. One very important thing that we forget individually and as a society is that unhappiness is a great motivator for change, growth, and progress. It is *not* during times of contentment that we make our greatest strides—it is our times in the fire that propel us forward into new realities. When we start avoiding and anesthetizing ourselves from the "darker" ranges of feelings, we lose touch with one of the greatest influences on our personal and collective progress. In the natural world and in our lives, too, there is a time and place for all extremes of expression. When we cut ourselves off from half of our feelings, we go against the nature of things and our own best interests. When you allow and embrace all of your feelings—even the "dark" or painful ones— you strengthen your spiritual resilience and plant the seeds that will eventually grow into the happiness on the other side of the hit you've taken.

* * *

Bounce Back Boot Camp

Here are some spiritually empowering substitutes for numbing yourself:

- Sometimes grief, anger, or sadness is so overwhelming that you feel as though you cannot tolerate it. In your most difficult moments, remind yourself that it is these times, especially, that bring you closer to the end of your time in the fire.
- When the pain is very bad, focus on small things that will center and calm you. Notice your feet on the ground. Walk barefoot and concentrate on the feeling of the floor or earth—feel your connection to the earth and let gravity remind you that you are being held by a force larger than yourself. Focus on your breathing. Feel the breath enter and leave your body, noting its passage through your nose or mouth, into your lungs, and back out again. Visualize the oxygen you have drawn in as it makes its way to your fingertips and toes, nourishing all your tissues as it makes its journey. Let this remind you that you are continuously being nourished by a universe that loves you and will sustain you.
- Even though your energy may be very low, consider exercising as a healthy substitute for numbing. Running, brisk walking, and yoga are particularly good. It is our experience and that of many clients that exercising provides a much-needed release from painful feelings and also gets your body's natural painkillers, endorphins, mobilized. One way to motivate yourself to exercise when it is the last thing you feel like doing is to give yourself permission up front to do it for just five or ten minutes. Even that small time can be tremendously beneficial, and chances are, once you've started, you'll want to keep going a little more.
- Pray or meditate. Praying aloud can be particularly effective. Consider *asking* for divine intervention and solace.

Asking for help out loud sends powerful signals out into the universe but also deep into your unconscious mind, which contains a reservoir of resiliency just waiting to come to your aid. If you have a hard time praying or meditating, use a tape or CD with a guided meditation. (Check out our website for information about guided meditations and for links to other helpful resources.)

- Try an activity that requires using your hands, like knitting or whittling. The repetitive motions, especially when combined with prayer or music, are very comforting.
- Sit in a rocker or a glider and let the motion soothe you. Swings and hammocks are also very helpful. Remember that your body assists your mind and heart to heal.
- Have healthy and delicious foods and drinks on hand during your time in the fire. Ask a friend or family member to help keep you nourished. Fresh fruits and juices will give you much-needed vitamins, and nuts and olives provide healthy fat—have appealing options around so that you can make empowering choices.
- Fill up your senses. Light scented candles. Burn incense. Sit by a roaring fire. Listen to music. Let your senses help you feel *more* and remind yourself that the more you feel, the faster you heal.
- Repeat (and write on a notecard and display somewhere you can see it throughout the day) this little prayer written by Dame Julian of Norwich, a fourteenth-century mystic:

> *All shall be well,*
> *and all shall be well,*
> *and all manner of thing shall be well.*

When you feel like escaping or anesthetizing yourself, remind yourself that even though it seems impossible during this time in the fire, all really *shall* be well.

• • •

Bring in the Troops

I get by with a little help from my friends.

—JOHN LENNON

ONE REASON WHY SPIRITUALLY BULLETPROOF PEOPLE ARE ABLE TO take any hit and come out on top is that they seek support during times of crisis. They derive this support in a variety of creative and inspired ways and use it like high-octane fuel to power themselves through their hits to the happiness that is waiting on the other side. Spiritually fragile people often have much less support while they're down-and-out, and this makes it a lot harder for them to rebound. Resilient people are typically more successful in getting the support they need because they hold certain beliefs and engage in certain behaviors that work in their favor. By adopting these beliefs and behaviors, you can send your resiliency soaring, too.

When comedian Drew Carey jokes "Oh, you hate your job? Why didn't you say so? There's a support group for that. It's called

EVERYBODY, and they meet at the bar," the audience laughs because, on a certain level, we're all in the same boat. We all have problems and pain in our lives, we all want and need support, and we all try to get it any way we can. But when you've taken a heartbreaking hit, the need for support is no laughing matter—getting it makes all the difference in being able to bounce back. While spiritually fragile people often struggle with inadequate support in times of crisis, spiritually bulletproof people are willing to receive and are resourceful

> Spiritually bulletproof people are willing to receive and are resourceful in finding the support and assistance they need.

in finding the support and assistance they need.

Resilient people are often very creative in their approach to life, and when they've taken a hit, they apply this creativity to gathering the support they need to come out on top. They think outside the box and find sources of support that others might forget about, dismiss, or never even think of. They also are good at maintaining their sources of support over time because they are realistic about and respectful of other people's lives and limits. If you can become more comfortable with and skillful at "bringing in the troops," you will significantly improve your odds of bouncing back.

Support Saboteurs

There are lots of things that can get in the way of getting the support you need when you're in crisis. Take a look at this list of attitudes and behaviors that can sabotage your ability to get the assistance you need and see if any of them apply to you:

- I feel the need to present an "I-have-my-act-together" image to others at all times.

- I believe that asking for support puts a burden on other people in my life.
- I'm afraid that asking for help will make me appear weak or unattractive to others.
- I'm nervous about showing my vulnerabilities to others because I think they'll like me less or use them against me someday.
- I just wish someone could solve all my problems for me or make them go away.
- I feel like all my family and friends are sick of hearing about my crisis.
- I think that letting me "vent" about my problems is the best way for people to support me.
- I depend on one or two people for all of my support.
- I don't want to have to figure out new ways to get support.
- I don't want to talk to strangers about what I'm going through.

Do you recognize yourself in any of these statements? Getting support is not just a matter of luck—it's a skill that can be learned like any other. You can become adept at "bringing in the troops" if you are willing to let go of some limiting beliefs you may have and begin to do some new things to help yourself.

The Friends and Family Plan

One of the cell phone companies used to have a calling plan that allowed you to call anyone on your "friends and family list" for one monthly price, no matter how long you talked or how many calls you made. While this might be a good plan for saving money on your cell phone, sticking with your "friends and family list" when you're trying to find support during a crisis will probably cost you, in more ways than one. When Anna was going through a terrible divorce and custody battle, she started to feel as if her friends became less and less available over time. At first, her friends made themselves available to her for long conversations and late-night vent sessions, but as the months wore on, Anna noticed that she was getting answering machines more and more and that when she did reach someone, that friend was usually running late for something or running out the door. She started to feel angry and abandoned by the very people she thought should be there for her during times of trouble. What Anna didn't understand was that her need for support went beyond what her friends were able to offer. Because they didn't know how to tell her that they were tapped out, they just started becoming less available.

Anna's situation is extremely common among people who have taken heartbreaking hits—they rely heavily on family and friends and don't find alternative sources of support. We understand that it's natural to want to talk with the people you're closest with and you *should* connect with those people. But many times, the people we know and love have lives and limits that make it impossible for them to be our primary sources of assistance. It is unrealistic to expect your family members or friends to give you all you need during this time in the fire. People have very busy lives and lots of their own problems—it's asking too much to want a relative or friend to serve as your personal therapist. More important—and please let this sink in—the people you're closest to may not have the right set of qualities, skills, experiences, and beliefs to offer you optimal support. This is important enough to say again: Even though you're probably most comfortable seeking support from your family and friends, it is very likely that they are not going to be able to give you all the assistance you want and need. This doesn't mean that you shouldn't make efforts to connect with those people, it just means that you might want to consider branching out. While you're in the fire, friends and family are wonderful sources of love, companionship, and conversation, and all of these things will help you weather the storm. But using every conversation and visit with them to work through your pain, anger, or loss is not the most productive way to bounce back and it puts a lot of strain on even your strongest relationships.

If this makes you feel worried, sad, or stressed because you don't know what else to do to help yourself or where else to turn for support, please take a deep breath and relax. You are not and will not be alone through your time in the fire—there are so many things you can do to make sure that you get the support you need. Realizing the limits of friends and family is your first step in identifying other strategies to help yourself—ones that will make a huge difference in your ability to come out on top of the hit you've taken.

Finding Other Friends in the Fire

Spiritually bulletproof people are open to new people and are more likely than spiritually fragile people to agree with Will Rogers's famous line "A stranger is just a friend I haven't met yet." One of the most effective types of support available to you when you're in the fire comes in the form of "friends you haven't met yet." When you've taken a hit, don't underestimate or over-look the kindness of strangers. Resilient people are much more likely to connect with new people through support groups or through the Internet than are their more fragile friends. One of the most successful, ongoing support groups of all time is Alco-holics Anonymous. This organization has helped millions of people beat their addictions in large part because it allows peo-ple to connect with and get support from other people who truly understand what they're going through. Even though the people who come to any given meeting may not have ever met before, they understand that they are friends in the deepest sense—they are in the same boat and share the same challenges. Since mem-bers' lives don't intertwine in other ways, it allows them to focus on supporting each other. Many support group members wind up feeling better understood and more deeply supported by relative strangers than they do by friends and family. There are certain kinds of pain and experiences that can only be understood by someone else who has also gone through them. When Azim goes and speaks with a group of newly bereaved parents, he can say things to them and offer support in ways that I cannot—he has stood in their shoes and is in a real position to offer valuable support. If I talk with a group of people who suffer from chronic pain, they know that I know what they are experiencing. We talk the same language and are running the same race. Spiritually bulletproof people derive tremendous benefit from connecting with others who share their experiences. There are support groups for almost every kind of hit. If you've been newly diagnosed with any disease, if you or someone you know is chronically ill, if you've lost your job, your child, your breast, your marriage, or your home, there are other people who know just how you feel and are waiting to meet you and support you. One of my friends, Mary Anne Pace, facilitates the adolescent bereavement support group for the local hospice chapter. Every Friday evening, she meets with a group of teenagers who have all recently lost a parent to cancer. She tells me that these kids really come to rely on their new friends in the group for support and that they can't wait till Friday night so that they can be with other people who really understand what they're going through. While their school and social friends are still needed for fun and companionship, support group friends can offer something that others simply cannot, no matter how much they want to help. If you want to really find fabulous support, consider taking the initiative to find a support group. It can be hard to take the initiative when you're hurting, but it is worth pushing yourself to do. Even if you don't want to leave your home, there are thousands of online support groups and chat rooms where you can connect, any time of the day or night, with other people who'll understand what you're going through. If you want to tap into your bulletproof potential, remind yourself that these strangers are really just friends you haven't met yet.

The Blessing of Books

How would you feel if you knew that you had at your disposal an army of great minds and souls just waiting to support you through your time in the fire? Just knowing that so many wise and experienced individuals had your problems and life in mind and wanted to offer their comfort and advice would probably make you feel a lot more supported. Spiritually bulletproof people are never without support because they understand the true nature of books. Books are not simple inanimate objects that carry information—they are energetic connections among their authors and every single person who has ever read them. Take a minute to read what some great thinkers have to say about the role of books in our lives:

> *When you sell a man a book you don't just sell twelve ounces of paper and ink and glue—you sell him a whole new life. Love and friendship and humour and ships at sea by night—there's all heaven and earth in a book, a real book.*
>
> —CHRISTOPHER MORLEY

> *I suggest that the only books that influence us are those for which we are ready, and which have gone a little farther down our particular path than we have yet got ourselves.*
>
> —E. M. FORSTER

> *Except a living man, there is nothing more wonderful than a book! A message to us from the dead—from human souls whom we never saw, who lived perhaps thousands of miles away; and yet these, on those little sheets of paper, speak to us, teach us, comfort us, open their hearts to us as brothers.*
>
> —CHARLES KINGSLEY

Medicine for the soul.

—inscription over the door of the Library at Thebes

When you are trying to bounce back from a bullet, calling in the troops to help you can make a huge difference. Begin to expand your ideas about possible sources for support. Spiritually bulletproof people feel connected to those who have come before them and walked the path of adversity, too. They know that love and help comes through to them in many forms, not just through actual living, breathing people up close and personal. They understand that they are not alone and that other men and women are always available to them through books and through other kinds of art, as well. Oprah Winfrey, a bulletproof spirit if there ever was one, started her famous book club largely because of the huge influence books had upon her while she was growing up and throughout her life, and she wanted to share that tremendous spiritual, emotional, and intellectual resource with as many people as she could. When you are trying to rebound from adversity, realize that books may be one of your greatest resources. Think about, as Henry David Thoreau writes, "How many a man has dated a new era in his life from the reading of a book," and realize how the love, wisdom, and energy of the great men and women who've come before you are reaching out to support you even as you read these words.

• • •

Bounce Back Boot Camp

Here are some suggestions for "bringing in the troops" when you need support:

- Ask friends and family to help you with more than just opportunities to "vent." Ask them to find a local or online support group for you. This is something practical and concrete that they can do for you and, believe us, they will be happy to do the legwork for you. They can search and check out different possibilities and direct you to the most promising places. Doing the nitty-gritty searching and evaluating is something your loved ones can do for you during this time in the fire. Let them.

- Call or visit your local library and bookstores. Talk to a librarian or bookseller and ask for help coming up with a reading list related to your crisis. You can also ask for book recommendations from people in support groups. (We also have a book list on our website that may be quite helpful.) Pick a few promising titles and borrow or buy them. Put these books by your bedside and keep one in your purse, briefcase, backpack, or car. Consciously tell yourself that these books are loving and wise friends who are supporting you during this time in the fire. Remind yourself that they were written by people whose intention was to give you assistance. Don't forget that these authors are not strangers—they are simply friends you have not met.

- During this time in the fire, remember that your "troops" also include the ancestors who have come before you and whose blood runs through you now. You have inherited strength and resourcefulness from hearty men and women who had lives with just as many challenges as you face, if not more. You stand on their shoulders as you endure this time in the fire. Think about all the generations of men and women whose lives have contributed to yours—never forget that you walk in their footsteps and are never truly alone.

CHAPTER 12

Take Charge of Your Space

Your sacred space is where you can find yourself again and again.

—JOSEPH CAMPBELL

SPIRITUALLY BULLETPROOF PEOPLE USE ALL OF THE RESOURCES AT their disposal to turn adversity into victory and they recognize that their physical space or environment can assist them in the process. To raise your own spiritual resiliency, you must learn to be resourceful. Train yourself to look both inward and outward for ways to keep yourself spiritually healthy and to help yourself recover when you do take a hit. Because of the innate interconnectedness of all things, the power of your surroundings to affect you—for good *or* bad—is undeniable.

Albert Einstein once remarked that "The environment is everything that isn't me." Your environment is the sum total of all the spaces, situations, people, and interactions that make up your life, and much of it is completely beyond your control. While they do not operate under the illusion that they can, or

> Spiritually bulletproof people see the wisdom of taking charge of their *space* by harmonizing and optimizing what they can.

that it's even desirable to, control their *environment,* spiritually bulletproof people see the wisdom of taking charge of their *space* by harmonizing and optimizing what they can.

They recognize that just as they need to care for their own bodies, they are also responsible for creating a healthy and supportive space around themselves. They consciously bring more light, life, beauty, and joy to themselves in practical little ways that are available to them.

Taking Charge of Your Space

When you have taken a heartbreaking hit, you can become so consumed with what is going on *inside* that you forget to focus energy on your space, which is really an extension of yourself. In fact, during times of grieving, loss, depression, or stress, it is common for people to let themselves and their space go to seed. If it is hard to get up and get dressed, it is certainly not going to occur to you to take extra-good care of your space. Think about this concept in terms of your body. When you feel most exhausted and run-down, you are least likely to want to prepare healthy meals, although it is precisely then that you would benefit most from them. Spiritually bulletproof people know that it is the times you feel *least* able to give a damn about your space that you derive the *most* benefit from attending to it. Take a minute to create a mental picture: Picture yourself in charge of caring for a small, sick child. She is feverish and weak. Imagine putting her in a fresh cotton nightgown and tucking her into a soft, quilt-covered bed. See yourself feeding her spoonfuls of homemade chicken soup and showing her picture books of her favorite animals. How does it feel to create this space for her? Do you see that creating this space is an act of love? Do you believe that what you've created for her impacts her ability to heal? Now imagine that the child is you. How do you feel in this space?

Spiritually fragile people do not give themselves the gift of this kind of supportive space. Feeling overwhelmed can prevent them from taking steps to nurture themselves and their recovery with harmonious and healing spaces. Of course, the irony here is that unsupportive spaces do nothing to alleviate their feelings of being overwhelmed. Sometimes people unconsciously believe that they are undeserving of living in nurturing, supportive spaces, so they sabotage themselves by being disorganized, tolerating clutter, or taking the path of least resistance and living in highly impersonal spaces that do not speak to their souls.

Taking charge of your space means different things to different people. While spiritually fragile people may think about how their space functions for activities like eating, sleeping, and entertaining, spiritually bulletproof people believe that their space's most important job is to support their *spiritual* health.

Creating Sacred Space

There are many ways to take charge of your space so that it supports your spiritual health—and in times of crisis, so it supports your healing. Secrets 8 through 11 explored how important comfort, order, and support are in the wake of any heartbreaking hit. This chapter is about moving beyond basic environmental triage toward creating a space that actively supports spiritual resilience.

The Native American author Sun Bear writes that "When humans participate in ceremony, they enter a sacred space." For most people, ceremony is something that they participate in outside of their own spaces. Weddings, baptisms, bar mitzvahs, and funerals happen in sacred places like churches, synagogues, and mosques. But for spiritually resilient people, ceremony is a way of living each moment. In China, the art of serving and drinking tea plays a major role in the culture. The tea ceremony connects the mundane with the sacred, and wherever it is performed—at the Emperor's Court or the kitchen table—the sacred space appears. A sacred space, then, springs from our intention to connect the everyday with the spiritual.

Spiritually bulletproof people consciously create sacred space for themselves. They do this as part of a spiritually healthy lifestyle, but they also know how important it is to do when they're trying to heal from a hit and come out on top. The worse the crisis, the more critical it is to give attention to creating sacred space. Just as there are many kinds of people and many approaches to spirituality, there are many ways to create sacred space. There is no "right" way to do this. Many people take cues from their own spiritual heritage, but just as many borrow from other spiritual traditions to come up with highly individualized spaces. The most important things to consider are (1) your intentions for the space and (2) how to make it personally meaningful for you. Here are some ideas to get you started:

- It's important to remember that the *process* of creating your sacred space is just as important as the final outcome. Taking the time and investing the energy to take charge of your space sends a major signal to your unconscious mind and to the universe. It says "I believe that I can heal and I am committed to my spiritual development." When Azim was working to heal from the loss of his son, the process of sorting through photos and creating a beautiful staircase gallery of framed images of his son was a powerful and transformative ritual.

- A sacred space can be a small altar or it can be your whole home. I consider my entire house to be a sacred space, although I do have designated areas for prayer, meditation, journaling, and other spiritually supportive activities. I look at every room and every little thing in them as opportunities to connect the mundane and the sacred. For example, I put affirmations for health *inside* my medicine cabinet, I place cherished family photos *inside* my children's closets to remind them how loved they are, and I put inspiring artwork, books, and mementos everywhere, even the bathroom.

- An altar is usually a small table where you can create a symbolic sacred space. I actually use the windowsill above my kitchen sink as a kind of mini-altar since I spend so much time there doing dishes and preparing meals. Some people associate altars with sacrifice or think of them as being strictly for religious buildings, but personal altars are simply places where you can remind yourself of your connection to Spirit. People from almost all faith traditions and people with no particular religious affiliation use altars and there is no one correct way to arrange one.

- Choose an area to create your sacred space. You may want to symbolically clear the area of any energies that don't support your spiritual intentions by "smudging" it with sage or burning incense to mark the space. Buddhists, Roman Catholics, and many other traditional faith paths use this symbolic tool—it's *not* strictly a new-age practice. Release any resistance you may feel to claiming a sacred space for yourself.

- Think about what you want to *do* in the space and let that guide you. If journaling helps you to connect with your spirit, then stock the space with paper, pens, and pencils that inspire you. Designate a special table or lap desk for your journaling. If you intend to meditate or pray, where will you do that? A prayer shawl or a meditation bench or pillow may inspire you to grow your practice.

- Make sure that the objects you include in your sacred space are personally meaningful and supportive of the resiliency you want. Do not make the mistake of filling up the space with clutter. Choose with discernment. Rosary or prayer beads. Fresh flowers. Sacred texts or spiritual books. Candles and music. Objects with personal symbolism for you—

shells, special stones or crystals, musical instruments. Iconic images—the crucifix, the Star of David, saints' portraits, mandalas, statues. It takes time to create a sacred space that is highly personal and authentic. Sometimes, the simpler it is, the more profound will be its impact on you.

- Will this space be a private one just for you or will you share it with others? Set boundaries if you feel it's necessary.
- Remember that, more than anything else, what creates the sacred space is your intention and attitude. Let the space come to serve as a symbol for the sacred space you carry *within* you wherever you go.
- Maintaining your sacred space is a kind of prayer or meditation all its own. Consider the time and energy you devote to it to be time and energy invested in your own spiritual health.

When you take charge of your space, you nurture your own spiritual resiliency and give yourself a springboard to help you bounce back.

• • •

Bounce Back Boot Camp

Try out these strategies for taking charge of your space:

- Walk through your home and pay attention to how you feel in different areas. Where are you most comfortable? Where do you feel most inspired? Where do you feel most stressed? Letting your intuition guide you, begin a process of *lightening*. Carry a laundry basket with you and give yourself permission to put anything that just doesn't feel right or good to you in it. Try to actually remove at least 15 things. Declutter or just free yourself from stuff that doesn't speak to your most authentic self. It doesn't really matter what you remove—the process of claiming your space is begun with this first activity, and this sets into motion a series of healing changes to come.

- Using your journal, brainstorm about people, relationships, and situations that do and don't support your sacred space. Your "space" extends out into the world, too, so begin to think about what out there isn't working for you. Make a list of relationships and situations that are extensions of your sacred space. Take a moment to bless each of them.

- As you take charge of your space, consider what you already have and what is easily and readily available to support you. Again, walk through your home with your laundry basket and, this time, collect any objects, books, artwork, or other symbols that feel spiritually supportive to you. Look for the beauty and the sacred in the ordinary— fruit, flowers, photos. Using your treasures, create a temporary altar on a small table or other surface. This is about playing and connecting with spirit. As you place each object, reflect on its meaning for you and feel your spirit strengthened by it.

If you are interested in learning more about creating sacred space, please visit our website, where you will find links and great information to help you in this process.

• • •

Part Three

. . .

BULLETPROOF
BREAKTHROUGHS

Invoke the Sunset Clause

The indulgence of grief . . .
the blunder of a life.

—Benjamin Disraeli

SPIRITUALLY BULLETPROOF PEOPLE GRIEVE LONG AND HARD ENOUGH to move through and past their grief and then they use their remaining emotional energy to fuel their continued spiritual progress. They let the sun set on their grief because they recognize that it's just the first of many steps and stages in the process of bouncing back from and coming out on top of a hit. Spiritually fragile people, on the other hand, often make the mistake of indulging in grief, self-pity, or feelings of victimization long beyond the ability of those states of mind to assist them in recovering. If you want to maximize your own spiritual resilience, it's critical that you "invoke the sunset clause," which signals to your soul and to the universe that you're ready to stop grieving. You'll bounce back a lot faster and much more fully if you recognize the right time to *stop* grieving and if you can summon the inner strength to start the journey away from your grief and toward the happiness that awaits you. It's as important to know the proper time to *stop* grieving as it is to know how to grieve properly in the first place.

Spiritually bulletproof people know when to stop grieving and when to start moving on to new stages in their own healing.

When Winston Churchill said "If you're going through hell, keep going," he revealed his own bulletproof attitude and also the wisdom of getting out of certain places or states of mind. While they don't avoid, rush through, or in any way short-change their own need to mourn the hits they've taken, spiritually bulletproof people know when to stop grieving and when to start moving on to new stages in their own healing.

This doesn't mean that they don't grieve or mourn fully—as we've already established, resilient people often spend extended periods in the fire of pain and loss after taking serious hits. But when they're done with their grief, they move on. This allows them to focus all of their energy on the other stages of healing that many spiritually fragile people never get to experience because they're stuck permanently in a stage that is meant to be temporary. When they let the sun set on their grief, they're also allowing it to dawn on a new day of their spiritual journey.

Extreme Grieving

While grieving is a necessary stage in the healing process, many people stay stuck in this stage permanently and completely stall their spiritual evolution. Grieving is meant to be a process that winds itself down and goes on to feed new stages of healing. If you are stuck in perpetual grief, you may be holding on so tightly to what's happened in the past that you'll never be able to open your arms and embrace the possibilities of the present. When your grief becomes a permanent condition, the future also collapses and all that remains is a nightmare you can't wake up from. Grief is meant to be a profound part of the healing process—but it is not meant to become your new identity. Read about one woman whose grief defines her totally:

Eve works as a waitress at a small-town diner. She's in her late fifties but looks older. We have the same conversation whenever I come in for a meal or a cup of coffee—Eve tells me about the death of her twenty-year-old son, which happened sixteen years ago. She cries every time we talk about her son, his death, or her life now. She has not moved a single item in his room, not even to make the bed that she found him in after he died in his sleep from a silent heart defect. She works at the diner so she can scrape by and pay her bills—she left her career in human resources after her son died and never wanted to go back. She tells me that she is in the same daily pain now as she was sixteen years ago and her marriage ended more than a decade ago when her husband wanted to start living again and she didn't want to join him. She goes home to an empty house and has very few friends because she can't enjoy any normal activities or have normal conversations. She tells me that the only thing she has to look forward to is dying, because then she'll be with her son again. Eve admits that she hopes that will happen sooner rather than later.

Now, read a profile of another parent who lost a son:

Azim works as a peace activist, teacher of forgiveness, and as president of a nonprofit organization he founded after his twenty-year-old son was murdered. He is close to sixty but looks younger. He talks about the death of his son with thousands of people a year and his mission in life is to help prevent the kind of senseless violence that claimed his son's life and put his fourteen-year-old killer away for fifty years. His work takes him into the workplaces, schools, homes, and hearts of all different kinds of people, and he teaches and learns many things every day.

He still misses his son terribly but uses his grief to fuel his own spiritual progress and to energize his work to make the world a more peaceful and loving place. He lives a full and happy life and enjoys his family and many friends all over the world.

He looks forward to continuing the work that his organization has pioneered and is excited about the day that his son's murderer is released from prison so that he can come and work for the nonprofit organization and use his own tragic experience to help other people. Azim believes that he will be with his son again one day and this is comforting, but until then, he has a lot of important work to do to help make the world a better place.

These two snapshots show us extreme ends of the grief-resolution spectrum and also make it clear that when there's no sunset on your grief, no new day of fulfillment and happiness can ever dawn. Obviously, most people fall somewhere between these two extremes and very few hits are as brutal as the death of a child, but anyone who has ever taken a serious hit knows what it is to grieve. Finding the right time and way to let the sun set on your grief requires awareness, wisdom, maturity, and self-discipline. It also requires a shift in perspective that allows you to look at this sunset as a beginning and not an end.

When Things Get Complicated

In most situations, grief is self-limiting—if you're like most people, you'll eventually move through the challenging emotions and stages within the grieving process and become ready to let the sun set on your grief. But certain people get "stuck" in their grief and cannot move past it. Sometimes this prolonged and overwhelming grief is what bereavement professionals call "complicated grief." Complicated grief after losing a loved one to death, divorce, or another heartbreaking hit is usually rooted in difficulties with or unresolved tension in the original relationship. Many times, people are grieving more for something they never had than for what they lost. Sometimes, unfinished business with someone can make it impossible to let the sun set on grief. Take a look at some of the signs of complicated grieving:

- Even after a prolonged period of mourning, you still have difficulty speaking about the person you lost without re-experiencing fresh and intense grief.
- You constantly bring up the subjects of death, divorce, or whatever hit you took in even the most casual conversations.
- You have sleep issues that persist for months and are not improving.
- You are acting in self-destructive ways—drinking too much, taking drugs, being promiscuous, or being financially irresponsible.
- You have a hard time being anywhere near anyone or anything that you associate with the person you're grieving for or the hit you've taken.
- You have extreme and persistent feelings of guilt, despair, and low self-esteem that are not improving.
- Even after a prolonged period of mourning, you cannot manage your everyday responsibilities at all.

If you recognize yourself in any of these statements, we urge you to connect with a bereavement counselor or other mental-health professional. If you cannot let the sun set on your grief and especially if you think you may be suffering from complicated grieving, please reach out for professional help. There are many loving and dedicated professionals whose calling in life is to assist people like you through stuff like this—do not waste one more day suffering alone. If you don't know where to start, go to our website, where you will find some resources to guide you.

If you are experiencing complicated grief, some of the secrets that we'll share next may be very important for you to read. For instance, it is our experience that forgiveness plays a profound role in being able to bounce back from many of the most difficult hits. Please keep reading and also let us know how you're doing by visiting us on the web and posting a message.

Sunset Saboteurs

Even if you're not struggling with complicated grief, you may still have a hard time letting the sun set on your grief. We've worked with many people over the years who *wanted* to move past their grief but felt unable to for certain reasons. It's very common for people to have certain misconceptions that get in the way of them moving beyond their grief. Here are some of the most common sunset saboteurs:

- You feel that to stop grieving would be disloyal. For instance, if you've lost a spouse, you may think that you're not honoring him or her if you let the sun set on your grief.
- You are afraid of criticism from other people. You may think that relatives, friends, or neighbors will think you're cold or deficient if you let the sun set on your grief.
- You may fear that your support will vanish if you stop actively grieving. You might worry that you will be left to deal with things all by yourself.
- You might have started to identify yourself with your grief. Maybe you have come to think of yourself as "the bereaved widower" or the "wronged wife." You might have gotten used to this identity and even enjoy some of the attention or sympathy you get. (This is very common and natural, so

don't get down on yourself if there's a little bit of truth in this for you.)

You may mistakenly believe that letting the sun set on your grief is the *end* of your journey, so you may be reluctant to let go of your grief because you think of it as all that remains of your pre-hit self or life. Don't you worry—you are at the *beginning* of an adventure that you were born to experience and you are about to discover that there's more to yourself and to your life than you ever knew was possible. We are honored to be sharing that journey with you and will be with you in spirit every step of the way.

• • •

Bounce Back Boot Camp

The following ideas will help you let the sun set on your grief:

- If you are ready to let the sun set on your grief, spend an evening watching the sun set. Make a production out of it—find out for sure when the sun will be setting, plan where you want to watch it, and set yourself up so that you can comfortably view this often-overlooked celestial event. Really watch the sun as it makes its journey toward the horizon and make sure you keep your eye on it as it slips away. As the sun sets on the day, state your intention to release your grief. Say something (out loud) like: *"I am ready to let the sun set on my grief so that I may finally rest and then awaken to a new day of healing in my life."*
- Write a letter to your grief, telling it that you're ready to let it go. Write as little or as much as you want to and then roll the note tightly and slip it into a balloon as you inflate it. On a windy day, go outside and release the balloon with your grief inside. As you watch it get smaller and smaller, feel your grief get smaller and smaller, too. (You can even do this exercise in your imagination. Lie in bed at night

and watch your balloon float away, taking your remaining grief with it.)

- If you feel more comfortable putting your grief away instead of releasing it, put your letter inside a small box and lovingly wrap the box as you would a gift. Tie a ribbon around the box and give yourself the gift of putting your grief away. Put the box up on a high shelf in your closet or in your attic. Know that you can always take it down again for a visit but also know that you no longer need to.

•   •   •

SECRET #14

The Real Meaning of the F-Word

*To forgive is to set a prisoner free
and find out that the prisoner was you.*

—Lewis B. Smedes

FOR SOME SPIRITUALLY FRAGILE PEOPLE, FORGIVENESS IS LIKE A DIRTY word. After being hurt or betrayed, they may actually be offended by the idea of forgiving the person or people responsible for the hit they've taken. They have a lot of misconceptions about forgiveness and these prevent them from using its power to help them bounce back from the bullets they take. Spiritually bulletproof people understand the profound power of forgiveness and make a personal commitment to practicing it in their lives. They understand that forgiveness is a gift to themselves because it can free them from the residual anger and pain left by life's heartbreaking hits. When you understand the real meaning of the "F-Word," you will send your spiritual resiliency through the roof.

Forgiveness is one of the most misunderstood concepts going, and because of this, it eludes us when we need it most. We're often told that we *should* forgive—that it will be good for us—but no one ever tells us exactly *how* to do it. The good news is that while forgiveness *is* miraculous, it is *not* a complete mystery. Although the hits they take may leave them with residual pain, anger, loss, and resentment, spiritually bulletproof people practice forgiveness and see it as the greatest gift they can give themselves.

> Spiritually bulletproof people practice forgiveness and see it as the greatest gift they can give themselves.

Forgiveness is actually *simple,* but it is not *easy* to do. You may find it hard to do at first because it is counterintuitive. Your logical mind will often resist the idea of forgiveness after you've taken a serious blow, but if you want to bounce back better than before, you can't let your brain boss you around. Albert Einstein was obviously as brainy as they come, but even he acknowledged the limits of the intellect—he thought that it was a useful tool, but warned against letting it lead. When you forgive, you must let your spirit lead. Your spirit is very good at forgiving—though you may not yet realize it—so all you need to do is peel away the layers of resistance that your mind has put between you and forgiveness. When you clear your mind of certain patterns of thinking, forgiveness will rush in like the tide. And when it does, you will find yourself standing on the other side of the hit that's been hurting you and holding you back from the happiness you deserve.

Indulge in Forgiveness

Don't choose to forgive because you *should* or because it is the *right* thing to do—do it because it is a highly efficient and turbocharged way of connecting with the happiness that lies beyond the heartache you've been experiencing. Carrying around pain, anger, and resentment can make you more miserable than the original offenses committed against you. When you forgive, it is so that *you* can put this burden down. Forgiveness is not a pronouncement you make or an outward gesture of reconciliation— it is simply a transition you make *inside* of yourself. This transition to forgiveness *will* benefit the world around you in unexpected and uncountable ways, but learning how to do it is not for or about anyone else. Forgiveness is a gift you give yourself when you're ready to bounce back from the bullets you've taken. Begin to reframe forgiveness as an indulgence you deserve rather than as an obligation to someone or something else.

Even though we forgive for ourselves, our forgiveness does end up impacting other people and the world around us in profound ways. I once heard a story about a man who wanted to keep his small son occupied so that he could get an important project done. The father saw a map of the world in a science magazine and he cut it up into a bunch of pieces and asked his boy to put the puzzle back together again—"That'll keep him busy for a good, long while," the father thought to himself. Well, his son returned in five minutes with all of the countries perfectly placed. The father, unable to imagine how the child had been able to complete the task so quickly, asked the boy how he had done it. "It was easy, Dad," he said. "On the back of each piece was part of a man's face, and so when I put the man together, the world got put together, too." When we forgive, we begin to put ourselves back together after being shattered by the hits we've taken, and when we put our inner selves back in alignment, the world around us also begins to come together in amazing ways.

Most of us agree that forgiveness is, theoretically, a good thing. The problem with forgiveness is that it is never theoretical— it is always something we have to do in the real world with real people. Real-life forgiveness proves to be much stickier for us, but there is nothing that works as profoundly and miraculously to heal even the worst traumas. When Archbishop Desmond

Tutu worked with then-President Nelson Mandela to bring healing to a South Africa divided and ravaged by apartheid, he championed what he called *The Third Way*—a type of justice that emphasized restoration rather than retribution. Though the atrocities, crimes, and human rights violations that occurred under apartheid seemed completely unforgivable, breaking the cycle of hatred and violence required a new way of thinking. The title of Desmond Tutu's 1999 book, *No Future Without Forgiveness,* says it all—without the miracle of forgiveness, there was no future for the people of South Africa. In recognition of his work in the area of political forgiveness, he was awarded the Nobel Peace Prize. If forgiveness can heal on so dramatic and massive a scale, it can certainly help you come out on top of the hit you've taken.

Taking Stock When You're Stuck

Spiritually bulletproof people use the power of forgiveness to free themselves of the residual pain, anger, and resentment that hits leave in their wake. They refuse to stay "stuck" in bitterness and negativity and realize that forgiveness is their way out. Ask yourself the following questions to see if you're stuck with feelings that no longer serve your best interests:

- Do you find yourself mentally replaying incidents or conversations or dwelling on past situations?
- Do you have trouble picking out Mother's or Father's Day cards because none of the sentiments feel appropriate? Do holidays bring up unsettling feelings?
- Do you feel intense mixed emotions for someone in your life? Do you love someone who drives you crazy?
- Does thinking about or talking about a certain person get you upset? Is it hard for you to be around a particular person?
- Do memories of your childhood or the past interfere with your present life?

- Are you estranged from someone? Have you written someone off or out of your life?
- Is it hard to fully enjoy your life because your past still affects you?
- Do you feel an emptiness or pain in the pit of your stomach when you think about a certain person or situation?
- Do you try to forgive, but it just doesn't seem to work?
- Are you sick and tired of carrying around the pain that someone else caused you?

If you answered "yes" to one or more of these questions, you are stuck in an emotional prison. Forgiveness offers you a way out of being stuck with emotions that are keeping you from bouncing back. Start to think about forgiveness as your own personal "get-out-of-jail-free card."

Forgiveness Fallacies

It is very normal to feel a lot of resistance to the idea of forgiving the people or situation that hurt you. We have worked with lots of people over the years who had lots of objections that they had to work through before they could forgive. We'd like to clear up a few common fallacies about forgiveness that are at the heart of many of those objections:

- When you forgive, you are not forgetting or repressing your feelings—you are making a conscious choice to end your own suffering and to begin healing.
- When you forgive, it doesn't mean that you forget.
- When you forgive, you don't have to pretend that nothing ever happened.
- When you forgive, you don't condone or excuse what happened.
- When you forgive, it doesn't mean that there are no consequences for the person who hurt you.

When you make the decision to forgive, you take a big step toward coming out on top of the hit you've taken, but when you've been hurt and can't forgive, you experience chronic reinjury. One woman we worked with jokingly called this phenomenon "the gift that keeps on giving." When she got sick enough of receiving it, she finally made the decision to begin healing herself through the power of forgiveness. If you're sick of hanging on to pain you no longer need, open your mind and heart to the possibilities that forgiveness offers.

Hanging Your Heart on a Hook

Many times during a workshop, a participant will ask something like "Why should I let someone off the hook so easily?" and we understand why this is so common a concern. We may think that there's virtue in not letting someone "get away with" an offense, but who can be truly happy while holding someone hostage on a hook? More important, the person we're really keeping "on the hook" is the one we see in the mirror. When we refuse to forgive, we hang our own hearts on this hook. A hook is a terrible place to be hanging around and the suffering we inflict upon ourselves there is completely avoidable if we are willing to look at forgiveness in a different way.

Remember that when you forgive, you are not forgetting— you are consciously choosing to remember in a different kind of way. This different way of looking at things will help you bounce back from the hit you've taken and protect you from more harm. Forgiveness offers you a refuge, a protection, and a safe haven from the insidious damage that unresolved anger and pain create in your body, mind, and soul. Forgiveness is not an event or even a feeling—it is a process. While forgiveness actually happens in an instant, the process of preparing for that moment happens over time. Azim often says that *forgiveness occurs when preparation meets grace.* Part of your preparation is learning a new way of remembering. At first, this new way of remembering will feel strange and counterintuitive to you, and it is natural for you to feel some resistance. When this happens, pause and remember how many of the things that are now easy for you felt difficult or uncomfortable at first. Remind yourself that just because something is uncomfortable at first doesn't mean you shouldn't do it. You don't need to commit to a lifetime of forgiveness right now—just be willing to try a new way and see what unfolds. Don't worry if you don't know *how* to forgive at this point—just make a commitment to doing it. The next couple of chapters will show you *exactly* what to do. All you need at this moment is the willingness to free yourself through the power of forgiveness. Start by making it your intention to forgive. The profound power of intention cannot be overstated—it sends a signal inward to the deepest, wisest part of yourself and outward into a universe waiting to assist you.

• • •

Bounce Back Boot Camp

Here are some suggestions for getting more comfortable with the "F-Word:"

- All you need to start is a willingness to forgive. Begin by stating that it is your intention to forgive. Write your intention down on a few Post-its and place them where you will see them as you go about your daily routine. The bathroom mirror, your bedside table, and the dashboard of your car are usually good spots. Every time you reread your new intention, feel your readiness to forgive increase.

- Begin to think about forgiveness as a kind of shelter that you can go to as an escape from the pain and loss you've been carrying around. Since shells are one of nature's perfect shelters, find a shell that you like and see it as a symbol for your new intention to forgive. Keep it on or near you as much as possible and let it remind you that forgiveness offers you a way to escape the pain your hit left in your heart and in your life.

- Visualize a beautiful place of shelter where you can retreat from all feelings of pain, resentment, or anger. Picture yourself in a large, white tent with billowing fabric and Persian rugs on the floor or imagine yourself in a rustic tree house, surrounded by towering pines and filled with dappled sunlight. Make your imaginary shelter your perfect refuge—give it as much detail as you can and bring it into perfect focus in your mind. Visit this shelter before you fall asleep at night and remind yourself that this is a place of total forgiveness.

• • •

SECRET #15

Learn the Forgiveness Formula

*The wise man will make haste to forgive, because he knows
the true value of time and will not suffer it to pass away in unnecessary pain.*

—SAMUEL JOHNSON

SPIRITUALLY BULLETPROOF PEOPLE FIGURE OUT HOW TO FORGIVE SO
that they can come out on top of their hits. Spiritually fragile
people misunderstand forgiveness and this makes it impossible
for them to let go of their negative feelings about the bullets
they've taken. Remember Desmond Tutu's book title *No Future
Without Forgiveness*? Well, you seriously undermine your *own* future when you can't forgive what's happened in the past.

You may want the release that forgiveness offers but have no
idea how to actually do it. It is hard to take on something as big
as forgiveness if your ideas about it are confused or vague. While
it may seem like they have something different or special about
them because they are able to forgive, the truth is that spiritually
bulletproof people understand that forgiveness can be learned
and that it is a practice, not an event.

Even though it's not always *easy* to forgive, it is actually a fairly *simple* process. The chapters that follow offer more forgiveness coaching, but let's begin with the basics—the formula we're about to share with you is straightforward and practical and will get you started.

> Spiritually bulletproof people understand that forgiveness can be learned and that it is a practice, not an event.

The Forgiveness Formula

Words are powerful—they carry meaning, intention, and energy. Sometimes one word can make all the difference in the world. Imagine if Martin Luther King, Jr., had addressed a quarter of a million people in our nation's capital and told them "I have an *idea* today" or "I have a *wish* today" or even "I have a *vision* today." Dr. King's *dream* started with the word itself and so it is that forgiveness starts with the word itself.

Take a look at how the word *forgive* has two parts:

for + *give* = *forgive*

The Forgiveness Formula is simple, but sometimes the simplest things are the most profound. Einstein's $e = mc^2$ is stunningly simple and it helped us see the universe in a whole new way. And anyone who's ever struggled through chemistry or trigonometry knows that a formula may help us remember something important but that it only comes to life for us when we understand the different parts of the equation. Let's look at the very simple parts of the Forgiveness Formula:

the prefix *for* means *before*

Think about the *foreword* of a book—it comes *before* the actual narrative. A weather *forecast* tells us if it will rain or shine *before* it actually does either. With this in mind, we see that:

to <u>for</u>give = to give <u>before</u>

To forgive is to give before or to give ahead of time. Giving ahead of time can feel counterintuitive at first—you're probably much more comfortable giving *after*. For example, you give your money to the restaurant after you've eaten the meal and you pay your hairstylist after you've had the haircut. If you're like most people, you're probably a little nervous giving ahead of time—it can feel risky. Giving ahead of time requires faith that, in the end, you'll get something in return. Sometimes, the only way to get something you really want is to give ahead of time even though it may require a leap of faith on your part. Take a look at this dynamic at work in your everyday life:

- When you invest your money, you give ahead of time. When you make an automatic deposit into a mutual fund or retirement account, you get nothing tangible other than a statement at the end of the month. When you take your money out from under your mattress, you are taking a leap of faith because there's always the chance that your investments will lose value. Sometimes your fear of such an outcome might tempt you to leave your money in a traditional savings account, but being able to tolerate some risk is essential if you want to make your money grow.

- When you smile at or say hello to a stranger in the doctor's waiting room or on line at the post office, you often end up having a lovely little exchange with a unique and interesting person. Giving ahead of time, even in such mundane circumstances, is still a tiny leap of faith because there's always that small chance that your sociability will be met with a grumpy glare or a curt reply. Sometimes your fear of such a reaction might stop you from reaching out, but you're not risking much and the rewards of giving ahead of time in this way can be great—you may find friends or learn things you need to know while waiting in all those lobbies!

In both of these situations, *giving ahead of time* pushes you out of your comfort zone—if only a little. Forgiveness also pushes you out of your normal comfort zone—to a greater degree. It takes awareness, commitment, and discipline but will reward you with super spiritual resilience. Forgiveness is one of the very best investments you will ever make. It *does* require a leap of faith, but it *will* pay off when you find yourself on top of your hit.

Giving Love Ahead of Time

When you forgive, what exactly is it that you'll be giving ahead of time? When you forgive, it simply means that you give love ahead of time. In practical terms it means that you give love:

- *before* you get an apology
- *before* you see any change in the other person
- *before* the situation improves
- *before* your anger subsides
- *before* you think it's deserved
- *before* you feel like it

It is entirely natural to feel a lot of resistance to the *before* part of this formula and the *giving love* part may push your buttons, too. It's very helpful to understand the following things about giving love:

- it can be a completely *internal* experience
- it is something you do for *yourself*—it is *not* about anyone else
- it does not require you to *say* anything to anyone
- it does not require you to *do* anything at all
- it has to do only with your own thoughts
- it is a discipline that can be learned

Love is not a feeling or even an action—it is a way of *thinking*. When you forgive by giving love ahead of time, your motivation for doing so is your desire to free yourself from the residual pain that is keeping you from coming out on top of the hit you've taken. When you give love ahead of time, you are consciously choosing to have faith that forgiveness will help you bounce back from the bullet that hurt you. Everything you think and do in this process benefits you directly and works to heal your heart and your life. The Forgiveness Formula is the *"for yourself" formula*—it works at every level and it will work for *you* if you learn it and practice it.

Stars and Beanstalks

It may be that the only way you ever understand something fully is through experiencing it personally. In his poem "When I Heard the Learn'd Astronomer," Walt Whitman contrasts listening to an astronomy lecture with the experience of going outside to gaze at the stars. Reading about forgiveness is a little bit like attending an astronomy lecture—you may encounter new ideas and get inspired. But to reap the benefits of forgiveness, you must experience it personally. Forgiveness is one of those experiences—like falling in love or giving birth—that cannot be adequately described. Once you experience the freedom of forgiveness, you'll never want to go back to the prison of holding on to your pain and anger. Just as you cannot really learn how to ride a bike without actually getting on one and riding, you cannot learn how to forgive without actually forgiving. That is why the Forgiveness Formula is so powerful—simply push through your resistance and follow the formula. When you are actually following the formula, you will *be* in the process of forgiving instead of just thinking or talking about it. You will also be in the process of bouncing back higher than you ever thought possible.

Practicing the Forgiveness Formula does require you to take a leap of faith. It can make you wonder if you're being foolish to let go of your anger or resentment when there's no guarantee that it will do anything good for you or make you feel better.

When you start to practice forgiveness, every logical part of your mind may rebel. But logic is not the most powerful faculty of your mind and it may prevent you from trying the one thing that will actually work magic. Do you remember the story of Jack and the Beanstalk? Who can forget poor, blundering Jack trading away his family's only cow for a few useless beans he believed were magical? His mother wanted the safety of a sure thing even if it meant barely scraping by, while Jack was fearless and full of faith and maybe a little foolish. But he was right to believe, wasn't he? From his tiny seeds of faith in the power of magic sprang a giant living ladder that reached beyond the ordinary world and all the way to the heavens. The answer to all of Jack's problems came when he invested all that he had before there was any logical reason to think it was a good idea. When you give love ahead of time, you're throwing magical beans out the window into the garden. As you do it, part of you might wonder if you're a fool for thinking it will work—*do it anyway.* When you forgive by giving love ahead of time, you are giving yourself the greatest gift of all.

• • •

Bounce Back Boot Camp

Here are some ideas for putting the Forgiveness Formula into effect:

- Buy some seeds and place a bowl of them on your nightstand or coffee table—you might even put a couple in your coat pocket or coin purse. Planting seeds is like forgiving—both require you to give ahead of time and have faith that your efforts will pay off. This visual, symbolic reminder will keep you inspired to take the leap of faith that forgiveness requires.
- Every time you feel a pang of anger, resentment, or upset about the hit you've taken or toward someone who wronged

you, immediately send that situation or person a loving thought. You do not need to feel loving feelings to begin. Just replace your negative emotions with a loving thought and send it out into the universe toward that situation or person. Practice thought-stopping and replace the thoughts that cause you pain with ones that soothe you and the situation. You are giving nothing up by doing this—just your own troubled heart and mind. You can say something like this in your mind: "I send love and positive energy toward _____ now." Notice how this makes you feel.

- Practice, practice, practice. The Forgiveness Formula is not something you do once and then get to forget—it is a *practice.* As your practice deepens and grows, you deepen and grow. Look for opportunities to practice forgiveness—they are everywhere. When someone cuts you off or grabs your cab, look at it as a chance to forgive. When a colleague or acquaintance is insensitive, practice your new method. Silently bless the people who offend you before they apologize, before they make amends, before you even feel like doing it. After you do this for a while, you'll never want to go back to holding on to your pain and punishing yourself.

• • •

SECRET #16

Realize with Your Real Eyes

Sin is whatever obscures the soul.

—André Gide

WHEN THEY'VE TAKEN A HIT, SPIRITUALLY FRAGILE PEOPLE TEND TO harshly judge the offending party or situation. They are often rigid in their positions—they look at things as being either black or white with no middle ground. This way of seeing creates a tremendous amount of internal discord and rules out the possibility of rebounding quickly. Spiritually bulletproof people are more nuanced in the ways that they see people or situations. They resist demonizing people or situations confronting them and this helps them respond to life's losses and disappointments with more resilience.

If you believe that a person or situation that hurt you is completely unforgivable, you will have a very difficult time coming out on top of the hit you've taken. The people or things you can't forgive will continue to hurt you. As Nelson Mandela points out "Unforgiveness is like drinking poison and waiting for the other person to die." If you want to tap into your bullet-proof potential, you need to learn a new way of seeing the people or things that you can't forgive so that you can stop poisoning yourself. Henry David Thoreau hits this nail on its head when he writes "It's not what you look at that matters, it's what you see." Even though the hits they take leave them with pain and anger just like anyone else, spiritually bulletproof people practice see-ing hurtful people and situations

> Spiritually bulletproof people practice seeing hurtful people and situations in ways that create inner harmony and make forgiveness possible.

in ways that create inner harmony and make forgiveness possible.

Like most of the secrets known to resilient people, this one hinges on transforming your own perception. It's all about changing the way you see people and situations—writer and painter Henry Miller had it right when he said "One's destina-tion is never a place, but a new way of seeing things." If you want to come out on top of the hit you've taken, you're going to need to release the residual pain that the bullets you've taken have left you with, and the quickest and best way to do that is by figuring out how to forgive. One trick that helps spiritually resilient peo-ple to forgive is that they make it their business to learn a new way of seeing people and situations that have hurt them. If you want to send your own resilience soaring, you must begin to transform your own perception—you must begin to "realize with your real eyes." George Bernard Shaw gets to the heart of this strategy when he writes "Better keep yourself clean and bright; you are the window through which you must see the world."

Beyond Black and White

One way that spiritually bulletproof people see differently from their less-resilient counterparts is that they are able to empathize with others, even when those others have hurt them. The true story that follows illustrates the relationship between empathy and forgiveness:

> *A man was traveling in Africa when his plane hit bad weather. The turbulence was so dramatic that the man began to fear that the plane might go down and that he might be killed. He had caught a glimpse of the pilot and copilot as he boarded and now found himself wishing that there were white men flying the beleaguered plane. He wondered if the black men in the cockpit could possibly be as competent as white pilots and he was anxious.*

Although this kind of thinking might shock us, we might be even more startled to learn that the man in the plane was Archbishop Desmond Tutu, Nobel Peace Prize winner and himself a black man. He tells the truth about his thoughts as a way of drawing attention to the power of conditioning to distort, thwart, or limit our perception, therefore causing us to act in damaging ways. Having grown up in South Africa, Desmond Tutu had been conditioned to believe in the inferiority of people with dark skin. He used this awareness of his own conditioning to try to understand why and how the white ruling class in South Africa did the terrible things they did during the apartheid era—he realized that he had been brainwashed during his childhood in much the same way that white children were. While he would never condone the atrocities and human rights abuses that occurred, empathy gave him a new way of seeing the sins of his countrymen—one that made forgiveness possible so that healing could begin. He expressed a deep and abiding faith in the core goodness of human beings while refusing to turn a blind eye to wrongdoing. He saw that people made major mistakes that couldn't be overlooked, but he didn't think that sins were unforgivable. This way of seeing helped him and his entire country to begin healing from one of the most horrific hits imaginable.

The Semantics of Sin

Spiritually fragile people often have difficulty forgiving what they consider to be the "sins" that other people have committed against them. If you judge something as a "sin," you might have a hard time forgiving it or the person who "sinned" against you. What do we mean when we use the word *sin*? Consider the biblical story of Jesus saving a woman accused of adultery from being stoned to death by saying "He that is without sin among you, let him cast the first stone at her." The crowd disperses because Jesus' statement allows each person there to recognize that he is not all that different from the "sinner" being judged and condemned. This story reminds us not to judge "lest we be judged," but it also invites us to a new understanding of what it means to "sin." If you want to conquer your crisis, begin to think about the "sins" that have been committed against you in a different way—one that makes it easier for you to free yourself from your own pain through the power of forgiveness.

We are *not* saying that people don't do bad—even horrifying—things. It's just that most of what we call "sin" and many of the things we refuse to forgive by unconsciously or consciously using that label need to be reexamined through the eyes of compassion and love. You don't do this for the benefit of other people who you think have sinned against you, but for *yourself,* so that you can more fully reclaim your own life through the healing that forgiveness offers. Seeing sin everywhere makes it impossible to bounce back from whatever it is that hurt you.

Both the Torah and the Bible refer to our "sinful" nature, but we have wrongly interpreted the word "sin." When we look to the ancient biblical languages of Aramaic and Greek, we learn that "sin" doesn't necessarily mean what we think it means. Sin may be better understood as:

- Missing the mark
- Making an error
- Immaturity or "unripeness"

Reframing your own "sins" and those of other people by substituting these more-accurate characterizations offers you a powerful way to help yourself bounce back from the blows you've taken. This new way of seeing is not intended to trivialize the wounds inflicted or the injustices committed against you. People can be so far off the mark that their actions are incomprehensible, errors can be extremely grave, and immaturity is often at the root of really dangerous and damaging behavior. However, you *can* get your brain around these new ways of understanding wrongdoing—who among us has never missed the mark, made an error, or exhibited immaturity that hurt someone else? Forgiveness depends on changing the way that you think about other people's wrongdoing, and transcending your hardships depends on this new way of interpreting what you see. It is possible to reinterpret the meaning of the past in such a way that you open whole new possibilities for the future. This is why forgiveness is miraculous.

The kind of seeing that sours your happiness and taints your joy focuses on sin—it makes other people "wrong" or "bad." When you choose to point to sin in others, you create a barrier to forgiveness and undermine your own resilience. How can your life or the world become happy places for you if you think they are filled with bad, wrong, and sinful people and things that cannot be forgiven? When you realize with your real eyes, you develop greater clarity so that you can see the truth about other people. If you want to bounce back from the hit you've taken, begin to see the mistakes that others make as part of being human and, therefore, as ultimately forgivable. Try to make your mind a place that offers "safe passage" to all the people who pass through it. Work with your own thought responses and practice controlling your own "attack thoughts" when someone who has hurt you passes through your inner landscape. Although this is a spiritual kindness to others, its main benefit is to you—do you really want to experience reality through a mind that is a dangerous place? Think about it.

• • •

Bounce Back Boot Camp

Here are some ideas to help you "realize with your real eyes":

- Look for little opportunities to practice this new way of seeing. Practice using new words and phrases for evaluating what you notice yourself judging. For example, when someone cuts you off on the highway, say something to yourself like "Wow, that person really made an error of judgment in doing that." If you don't like the way your sister-in-law's gossip stirs up trouble in the family, think to yourself "I think that Audrey is missing the mark when she talks like that. The way she talks is just a sign that she, like all people, is spiritually immature in certain areas." It will feel really silly and awkward when you first begin doing this, but it will become more natural over time. The way we think influences the way we talk, but the way we talk also affects the way we think. Begin by talking the talk.
- Sit down and make a list of three or four of your own actions that you're not proud of. For each one, examine how the wrong thing you did might be reframed as missing the mark, making an error, or as a sign or result of unripeness or immaturity. If you can see this about yourself, begin to extend this way of seeing to include people or situations that have hurt you.

- If there is someone that you need to forgive, actively discipline yourself to resist focusing on sin when you think of that person. When a judgmental or condemning thought arises in your mind, do not grab hold of it and hold it to the light like a color slide that you want to examine more closely. Practice noticing the thought only enough to put it aside just as you would put a slide back into a box.

- Keep a bowl of fresh fruit in your kitchen. Let it teach you about ripeness. While all fruit is *good,* not all fruit is *ripe.* When a peach is still too hard to eat, you do not say that it is *bad*—you wait for it to be *ready.* And so it is with people. Although *unripeness* may be a word and concept that is new for you, it is perhaps the most accurate way of seeing most of what you judge as sin. Oprah Winfrey is famous for saying "When we know better, we do better," and unripe is simply what people are before they know better.

• • •

SECRET #17

Partner with Your Inner Paparazzo

If your heart acquires strength, you will be able to remove blemishes from others without thinking evil of them.

—MOHANDAS K. GANDHI

SPIRITUALLY FRAGILE PEOPLE FOCUS ON THE FLAWS, FAILURES, AND deficiencies of other people around them, and this habit of taking negative mental pictures stunts their own spiritual resilience. Spiritually bulletproof people recognize their human impulses to find fault and look for the worst in others, and actively resist them. They increase their own spiritual strength and joy by cultivating the habit of catching others being good and looking for the best in the world around them. If you want to tap into your bulletproof potential, get conscious about the way you choose to see the people and situations that confront you on a daily basis. You can harness the powers of your own perception to help you heal after taking a hit.

When you've taken a heartbreaking hit, it is very easy to see the person or situation that has hurt you with deeply critical and condemning eyes. When you're suffering, your perception is often clouded by your own pain or anger. It is at these times that it is most important for you to practice seeing with your "inner eye," the wise part of yourself that's connected to your bulletproof spirit. Antoine de Saint Exupéry touches upon one of the secrets shared by resilient people when he writes "It is only with the heart that one can see clearly, for the most essential things are invisible to the eye."

> Spiritually bulletproof people consciously look for the best in other people and try to catch them being good.

While they are not naïve or blind to other people's faults or failures, spiritually bulletproof people consciously look for the best in other people and try to catch them being good.

If you want to bounce back from adversity, begin to cultivate a way of seeing other people that puts them in the best light possible. Walt Disney believed "Our greatest natural resource is the minds of our children," and if you want to connect with the profound power of your bulletproof spirit, realize that one of your greatest resources is the part of your mind that is still child-like in its innocence and nonjudgment of others.

Catch Them Being Good

The dictionary tells us that innocence is blamelessness or inexperience, but our bulletproof spirits tell us that it is the deepest truth about who we are. I once heard a bit of wisdom that I remind myself of all the time when I am with my own children—someone once told me that *you need to catch them being good.* The truth about our children is what we notice when we *do* catch them being good. Imagine what we would think of our kids if our opinions were based on their worst moments and their most difficult traits. Think about how damaging it would be to our children if we labeled them based on these low points rather than on the larger context of who they are. Take a moment to envision what someone could say about you if you were caught at your worst moments rather than your best. It's not a pretty picture, is it?

Speaking of pretty pictures, most of us have had the experience of cringing when we see ourselves looking decidedly *un-pretty* (or un-handsome!) in a photograph that is on display—remember high school yearbook pictures? Once I was at a retreat where I performed in front of a large audience. There was a photographer in the front row and she was sitting below me, looking up at me. It seemed that every time I opened my mouth, she would snap a picture. I have some experience working with photographers, so I knew that the combination of bad lighting, her angle, and her interesting sense of timing would create some pretty unflattering images of me. These pictures were going to be seen by a lot of people, and they were probably going to be the only ones most of those people would ever see of me, so I wasn't thrilled that the dental work on my upper left molar was going to be on such prominent display. Sure enough, when I later saw them on a website, I hardly recognized myself. That photographer had caught me at my absolute worst—the only good thing about it was that no one (other than my dentist!) would ever recognize me based on her pictures. I didn't like that she had missed an opportunity to capture something good about me. I laughed it off and moved on, but I made a point of noticing how it felt to be caught at my worst and have that image broadcast as the truth of who I am.

Catching people at their best is an art. Photography is a great example of the power of the one who perceives to reveal or distort the truth about the one being perceived. I love photography and have a special interest in portraiture because I also love people. I especially enjoy photographing my three children. Over the years, I have captured them from every angle and in every mood. My favorite photos are the ones that are really close up. I love catching them being beautiful. I take the time and make the effort to catch their best angles and their most endearing quirks. I delight in noticing and showing them how lovely they are. A few years ago, I finally listened to my lawyer and made a will and also wrote a letter to be opened in the event that I should die unexpectedly. In it, I asked my husband to help our children remember how I felt about them and what kind of mother I was by showing them all of the photos I had taken so that they could see through my eyes. The photographs I take of my children do capture something true about *them,* but they say more about *me* and how I see them.

All of your judgments are like photographs—they say more about you than they do about other people. Just as bad pictures of you don't reveal the truth about who you are, the judgments you make about the people who've hurt you do not capture the total truth of who they are. Judgment is catching people at their worst, and when you spend your energy judging others (even the ones who've hurt you), it makes it impossible for you to bounce back from the hits you take. The irony of judgment is that it is most damaging to the person who is judging. As you make the transition between judgment and forgiveness, you begin to see other people through different eyes. You start to see the wisdom of *catching them being good.*

Forgiveness and the Francesco Factor

When you snap a mental picture of someone else being bad, you get to feel—at least momentarily—that you are good by comparison. This need to find yourself good by comparison gives away your own hidden and misplaced guilt and compels you into a way of thinking that pushes that guilt off onto someone else— you may feel better temporarily but wind up feeling worse in the end. Fortunately, you can learn to see differently and with more love. There's a direct relationship between forgiveness and what I call the Francesco Factor.

Francesco Scavullo was famous for photographing some of the most beautiful people in the world. He considered it his calling to capture people at their very best, and his reputation for catching people at their most dazzling made him sought after the world over. He had a gift for noticing and highlighting what was lovely or special in each person on the other side of his lens. You have only to look as far as the supermarket tabloids to see that even the most beautiful people can look really, really bad in photographs. The paparazzi are so reviled because they delight in capturing the ugliest, most awkward and humiliating images of celebrities. Tabloid magazines are so popular because there is a part of us that wants to see others at their worst. When you make the decision to tap into your bulletproof potential, you need to become conscious of that tendency and resist it.

If you want to come out on top of the hits you've taken, remind yourself to partner with your inner paparazzo. People *are* what you see in the best pictures of them. They *are* what people notice about them when they're caught being good. Sure, they may sometimes appear or act in ways that don't live up to those finest moments and parts of themselves, but deep down at the core of who they are lies the beautiful, the good, and the lovable. You tap into your own bulletproof potential when you discipline yourself to see through the eyes of love. And while this new way of seeing is gentler on other people, remember that learning to see this way is something you do for *yourself.* Tap into your inner Francesco—begin noticing the beauty, goodness, and wisdom in other people. Practice focusing on the innocence at the center of each person, for here you find the deepest truth. This insistence on and consistent awareness of the reality of innocence will lead you to forgiveness. And when you can truly forgive the people and situations that have hurt you, you will find yourself on top of the hit you've taken and also on top of the world.

Bounce Back Boot Camp

Here are some ideas that will help you to partner with your inner paparazzo:

- Each night before you go to sleep, think of a person you want to forgive and imagine her as a small child. Picture this individual as a three- or four-year-old and notice the sweetness and innocence of her expression. Say silently "I see the reality of your innocence." You don't need to spend a lot of time on this—even thirty seconds of seeing this person's innocence will work magic.
- If possible, find an actual photograph of this person as a child and frame it. Place the picture where you can see it throughout the day and let it remind you of the true innocence at the core of this person.
- Learn to stop judgmental thoughts in their tracks. Use thought-stopping to break these old and damaging mental patterns. Whenever you catch yourself thinking in a judgmental way, put your hand up as if you were stopping someone walking toward you and say something like "Cancel that." This technique is very powerful—when you don't allow yourself to react in old and damaging ways, your brain will create different neural pathways that will eventually become your new and more-resilient default mode. Don't get angry at yourself and don't worry if you forget sometimes—just try to use thought-stopping as much as you comfortably can. You will be amazed at the transformation you will see after just one week of using this technique.

Practice Good Spiritual Hygiene

Spiritual hygiene is mindful attention to developing and sustaining a relationship with ourselves as spiritual beings.

—DEAH CURRY

SPIRITUALLY BULLETPROOF PEOPLE UNDERSTAND THAT IN ORDER TO take life's heartbreaking, mind-boggling, and gut-wrenching hits and come out on top, they must keep themselves in prime spiritual condition. They take care of their spirits through things like prayer, meditation, and mindfulness in much the same way that they maintain their physical bodies with things like nutrition, exercise, and cleanliness. They develop "spiritual hygiene" routines that keep them spiritually hearty and, therefore, much more likely to bounce back from the inevitable bullets that come their way. They don't wait until bad things happen to consider their souls' needs—they are constantly building their spiritual stamina and reserves so that they have something to draw upon when crisis or adversity strikes.

While they make efforts to stay strong and healthy in all the areas of their lives, spiritually bulletproof people make it a top priority to develop and maintain practices and habits that support their *spiritual* well-being.

> Spiritually bulletproof people make it a top priority to develop and maintain practices and habits that support their *spiritual* well-being.

This doesn't mean that they neglect the other aspects of the body/mind/soul connection; in fact, spiritually resilient people also tend to be in better physical, mental, and emotional shape than their spiritually fragile counterparts. But they really do give special attention to maintaining their souls' alignment, and this can make a huge difference when they get blindsided by misfortune or loss. In fact, Azim says that part of what helped him survive the loss of his son was that he had been practicing good spiritual hygiene in the years leading up to this tragedy. When he needed to find the inner resources to keep going in the face of incredible loss and grief, he could tap into the reserves of resilience that he had spent years of his life building up through regular prayer and meditation.

If you have been neglecting the needs of your spirit, please, *please,* don't beat yourself up. First of all, most of us have never been taught how to practice good spiritual hygiene, and second, the pace and demands of modern life make just getting through the day challenging enough! Forget about how you've managed your spiritual needs in the past—now is the time to realize that you deserve to indulge in fabulous and luxurious spiritual hygiene so that you can handle any hit that comes your way. The chapters that follow will give you lots of ideas for ways to feed your soul and strengthen your spirit. There are also many excellent books, websites, and teachers that can help you develop a spiritual hygiene routine that works for you. Check out our website to find more information and great links to get you started. When you make spiritual hygiene a priority in your life, you will be amazed at how super spiritually resilient you will become.

Mental Floss

If you're like most people, the word hygiene probably conjures up embarrassing memories of junior high health class or makes you think of deodorant. But the word hygiene actually just refers to conditions and practices that promote or preserve health. Hygiene is sort of a funny word, but it's a good word for our purposes here because it reminds us that our spiritual health is something that we need to *maintain* and pay attention to just like we do our personal grooming. We could use the words *wellness* or *health* or *maintenance,* but the word *hygiene* really lets us know that spiritual resiliency depends upon us taking care of our spirits on a daily, ongoing, and comprehensive basis. Just like dental floss can help you maintain a healthy smile, spiritual hygiene is a kind of "mental floss" that helps you maintain a healthy spirit.

It may be difficult to imagine, but just a few generations ago, people really didn't know much about or invest much energy in maintaining their mental health. There wasn't a whole lot of knowledge about how the mind functioned or what conditions it needed to thrive. Exactly a century ago, in 1908, the modern mental hygiene movement emerged as a result of strong public reaction to Clifford Beers's controversial autobiography *A Mind That Found Itself,* which chronicled his experiences in what were then called institutions for the insane. People with afflictions that would be easily treatable by our standards were often committed to these asylums and left to wither away.

Now, a century later, no one questions the importance of promoting and preserving mental health. Taking care of our minds is practically a national pastime—what would we do without Dr. Phil, Prozac, and mental health days? While no one questions the need for *mental* hygiene anymore, there are an awful lot of people walking around desperately in need of *spiritual* hygiene. While there are more resources than ever before to help you take care of your spirit, modern life is also constructed in such a way that when something's gotta give, the thing that often gets sacrificed is proper and adequate spiritual hygiene.

Don't Just Sit on Your Assets

Recently, I arrived a few minutes early at the radio station where I was about to be a guest on a talk show. The automotive expert on the air before me was urging listeners to educate themselves about how to maintain their cars, especially during the winter months. "After all," he reminded his audience, "your car is your second-biggest investment, right after your home." As I listened to the many callers ask their questions, I was amazed at how much time and energy people are willing to invest to keep their cars running smoothly, but it also made me sad to think about how little time and energy most people invest in keeping their spiritual selves running smoothly. And while your car and your home may, in fact, be your biggest financial expenditures, they are certainly *not* your most valuable assets. Spiritually fragile people often make the mistake of maintaining everything in their lives except their own spirits. They put more energy into caring for their cars than they do into caring for their own souls, and this kind of self-neglect diminishes their ability to rebound when the inevitable hit comes along.

Are You Too Busy to Brush Your Teeth?

If you don't make time to take care of your spirit's needs, you are far from alone. Most people are so busy just trying to get through the day that they don't even think about their own spiritual hygiene. See if you recognize yourself in any of the following scenarios:

- I never have a minute to myself. I crave a little solitude, but work, family, friends, and other obligations pull me in a million different directions.
- I wish I could find the time to pray or meditate, but my schedule is so jam-packed that I really can't fit one more thing in.
- I find myself feeling scattered or anxious a lot. I have a hard time getting centered.
- I worry all the time. Even when I go to bed at night, it's difficult for me to sleep because I can't stop thinking about all the things I have to deal with.
- I'm not really into going to church, but I would like to feel more of a connection with my spirit. I don't know what to do to take the next step.
- The spiritual tradition I was raised in doesn't really feed my soul, but I haven't found any other path that feels authentic to me.
- A lot of the time, I walk around feeling like a machine. I feel numb.
- I do find a real sense of peace doing yoga (or other spiritual practice), but I feel guilty taking the time away from my family.
- I am often impatient or irritable. I have a short fuse lately.
- I am overserious. I don't have time to play, and whenever I try to relax, I think of a million things I should be doing instead.
- I have a subtle feeling of fear or dread that I push down as much as possible by keeping busy.

If you find yourself agreeing with any of these statements, you need to devote more attention to your spiritual hygiene. If you feel that you cannot fit this kind of self-care into your life, remind yourself that spiritual hygiene is really one of the best investments you can make in yourself and for yourself. It is also one of the least-selfish things you can do because it will directly benefit all the important people in your life. When Mahatma Gandhi looked at his schedule for the day and saw that he was especially overwhelmed with tasks and appointments, he made doubly sure to fit in the time for meditation because he knew that it would actually help him get through all he needed to accomplish.

High Maintenance

We all have our own nighttime routines. Some people brush and floss their teeth. Some people wash and then apply cream to their face. Some people do all of these things. Personal hygiene is not a one-size-fits-all affair, and neither is spiritual hygiene. Finding an effective and authentic way of maintaining your spirit is one of the most important tasks of maturity.

If you don't feel that you have time to indulge your spirit's needs, consider the fact that a little spiritual hygiene now may save you a lot of downtime in the future. The reason why young people usually bounce back more quickly and fully from injury or surgery than older people is that they are usually in better shape to begin with. Studies show that older people who maintain a healthy weight and exercise regularly are also much more likely to make a full recovery after major surgery than are their less "maintained" peers. Similarly, people who practice excellent spiritual hygiene are able to bounce back from the bullets they take much faster and higher than people who neglect their spiritual well-being. Begin to think of spiritual hygiene as a kind of preventative maintenance that will give you the confidence of knowing that you can come out on top of the hits that come your way.

The Best Investment You'll Ever Make

While there's no question that taking care of your body and guarding your health is a smart move, there's also no getting around the fact that your body is a depreciating asset. No matter how well you care for your body, its strength and stamina will eventually decline. But when you practice excellent spiritual hygiene, it is entirely possible for your spiritual health to improve over the course of your life. Think about it—your spiritual strength and stamina can actually continue to increase throughout your life! Any investment advisor will tell you that it's smarter to invest in an appreciating asset than a depreciating one, so start to invest regularly in your "spiritual bank account." Then, when you need to make a withdrawal because you've taken a heartbreaking hit, there will be something in there to sustain you.

Any Given Sunday

On any given Sunday over the last seventeen years, until he retired this past year, NFL quarterback Brett Favre found himself on the football field starting for the Green Bay Packers. He had been in the NFL almost as long as some players have been alive and currently holds most of the well-known NFL records for quarterbacks, including most NFL MVP awards. Favre has taken his share of hits over his career. In his senior year of college, he almost died in a car accident and had to have 30 inches of his small intestine removed. A number of years later, he was diagnosed with avascular necrosis, the same degenerative hip condition that ended Bo Jackson's career. And in 2005, his family's home was destroyed by Hurricane Katrina. He has been sacked well over 400 times in the course of his career. This man really knows how to take a hit and come out on top! What's his secret?

While Favre makes it all look easy on the field, the key to his resilience year after year is the way he trains in the off-season. He is known for investing tremendous time and effort in preparing himself to be able to take any hit and bounce back. He shows up for training camp in stellar shape, and all of his investment pays off as the season unfolds. You may only see Favre on TV on Sundays, but you can be sure that maintaining and strengthening himself is something he does almost every day of the week—week after week, month after month, year after year.

In the big game of life, you are the quarterback making the big plays. No matter how carefully and well you play the game of life, there is no way to avoid getting sacked. In fact, you'll probably take a lot of hits if you're really out there playing your best. Regular training in the off-season is the best way for you to keep yourself spiritually strong so that you can take these hits and stay in the game. Think of spiritual hygiene as the training you do in the off-season so that, like Favre, you can stay in the game for the long haul.

* * *

Bounce Back Boot Camp

Many of the chapters that follow offer you support and strategies to help you practice better spiritual hygiene, but here are some ideas to get you started right away:

- Decide to develop one small spiritual habit that you will practice on a daily basis. It can be as simple as saying a teeny-tiny prayer of thanks every time you drink a glass of water to help you grow in gratitude for the simple blessings in your life. One little habit I practice is taking a few moments before I put my feet on the floor each morning to center myself and ask God to use me for the highest possible good throughout the day. No matter how late I may be running, I never skip this little part of my spiritual hygiene—taking thirty seconds won't make me any later, but it will get me started on the right foot. Check out our website for inspiration for developing and strengthening your spiritual habits.
- Consider setting aside one day or even a few hours every week strictly for spiritual maintenance. The idea here is to really reconnect with your spirit in an authentic way—not

just to go through the motions of some tradition that doesn't really speak to your soul. Some people use their day or time to attend religious services and have family time. Others may decide that spending time connecting with nature better feeds their souls. There is no one right way to connect with your spirit—the important thing is to find a way that is authentic for you. There are lots of great ideas for keeping a holy day or Sabbath—again, check out our website for some inspiration and helpful resources.

- Put a spiritual symbol of some sort—a small statue, a string of prayer beads, a picture of a saint, even an object from the natural world like a shell or special stone—in your medicine cabinet so you'll see it whenever you do your personal hygiene routine. Let it remind you that your spirit deserves your attention just as much as your teeth, fingernails, and split ends do.

- Your inner spiritual world and your outer material world are equally important. Do something every day to enhance both these worlds.

• • •

Part Four

. . .

A BULLETPROOF
BLUEPRINT

Dance Between Desire and Detachment

If you care enough for a result, you will most certainly attain it.
—WILLIAM JAMES

How helpless we are, like netted birds, when we are caught by desire!
—BELVA PLAIN

IF YOU WANT TO BEGIN REALLY ACTING FROM THE WISDOM OF YOUR own bulletproof spirit, you must learn to embrace one of life's most profound paradoxes: You must figure out how to combine *passionate desire* with *dispassionate detachment*. This dance of desire and detachment requires grace and practice but will reward you with a tremendous boost in your ability to bounce back after taking a hit.

Spiritually fragile people are often unaware of how important their desires really are to the manifestation of their dreams. They may also be rigidly attached to things turning out exactly as they want them to. Resilient people understand that they must learn to simultaneously harness the power of their desires *and* practice detachment from outcome if they hope to find the happiness that lies beyond the heartache that comes their way. Though it

> Spiritually bulletproof people combine the creative power of their desires and the profound power of detachment to heal from their hits and manifest their dreams.

takes daily practice and commitment, spiritually bulletproof people combine the creative power of their desires and the profound power of detachment to heal from their hits and manifest their dreams.

If you can cultivate the ability to embrace what, at first, may strike you as irreconcilable energies, you will possess a kind of security so deep that no hit will seem quite as scary to you again. This one secret can take you to a whole new level of bulletproof, if you're willing to expand yourself to accommodate it.

The Desire Debate

If you're like most people, you may feel ambivalent about your own desires. Your own collection of self-help and inspirational books may even make you question the desirability of desire. On one hand, you've probably read that desire is the energy that attracts people, events, and circumstances into your life. That's got to be a good thing, right? On the other hand, maybe you've read somewhere that desire is actually the root of all human suffering. And that's a bad thing, isn't it? Should you put energy into and focus upon your desires or should you try to eliminate your desires? The desire dilemma is enough to make you dizzy and disoriented!

Merriam-Webster's dictionary defines *desire* as "wishing, wanting, craving, or having a longing." The word *desire* also implies strength of feeling and strong intention or aim. Desire is more than just wishing or hoping for something, someone, or some outcome; it is a heady cocktail of thought, emotion, and intention. When you combine and focus these thoughts, emotions, and intentions, you absolutely begin to affect the people, things, and circumstances that you attract into your life. This is why your outer reality is, in part, a manifestation of your inner reality.

Desire is a force powerful enough to affect your destiny. Not realizing the power of your own desires is like trying to drive a car without understanding what a steering wheel is for. Someone who really knows his way around a steering wheel is Indy 500 legend Bobby Unser. Bobby believes that "Desire . . . is the one secret of every man's career. Not education. Not being born with hidden talents. Desire." And while desire may be an important key to a successful career, it is also one of the keys to successfully manifesting *anything* in the material world.

Make no mistake about it, your desires—as channeled through your imagination, thoughts, intentions, and words—flow out into the universe and attract things, people, and circumstances. Your desire is never "doing nothing"—it is always working for or against your highest good. Rhonda Byrne's recent best-selling book *The Secret* is a timely reminder of what the great teachers, sages, and mystics have been telling us for millennia. From Ralph Waldo Emerson to Mahatma Gandhi, from Florence Scovel Shinn to Wayne Dyer, the master teachers all point to the creative power of desire and intention. And when you are trying to overcome your particular hardship, tapping into the creative power of your desires is especially essential.

When you've taken a serious hit, it's likely that your dreams for yourself or your life have been shaken, shredded, or shattered. You might be afraid to let yourself desire or dream again after what you've been through. It's a bit like getting back into the stock market after you've lost serious money—you know it's the only way for you to achieve your long-term financial goals, but you are also understandably gun-shy. But in order to fully heal, you must find the courage to reenvision and reinvest in your dreams so that they may become manifest. You've got no choice but to jump, yet again, into that great stock market of life, knowing the risks but with faith in your chances.

Many people are unaware of or unwilling to act upon the truth that their own thoughts, intentions, and desires are the currency with which they purchase their future. Your desires are like the seeds a farmer plants in anticipation of the crops he hopes to harvest or like the stones a mason uses to build the foundation for the house in which he hopes to dwell—they are the internal blueprint for the external reality you're creating. Once you accept the immense power of your own desires to affect your destiny, you'll naturally want to do all you can to master your mind and harness the power of its desires.

La Dolce Vita

After you've taken a heartbreaking hit and have moved through the processes of grief and, if necessary, forgiveness, a perfectly simple and simply perfect question to ask yourself is "Now that some of the dust has settled, what is it that I really *desire*?" Often, the answer to that question will lead you somewhere beyond your former dreams and toward a destiny you may not even be able to imagine. Sometimes, it will lead you toward a place inside of yourself—you may find that what you really desire is to express or develop some aspect of your personality that has been undercover. Sometimes it will lead you to a place out in the world—a new career, a different apartment, a return to school. And I've noticed that in a lot of books I like, the asking of this simple little question seems to lead straight to Italy as the heroine goes in search of her own version of *la dolce vita,* or the sweet life. In Frances Mayes's soulful book *Under the Tuscan Sun,* she recounts how the heartbreaking hit of her failed marriage leads to the discovery of her passionate desire to live in Tuscany. Allowing herself to follow her desire requires bravery in the face of her fears but leads her to a destiny beyond what she imagined possible for herself. In Elizabeth Gilbert's lovely and spiritually rich memoir *Eat, Pray, Love,* the author finds that her desire to live in India, Indonesia, and—yes—Italy leads her from the heartaches inflicted by a painful divorce and broken love affair toward a destination inside of herself, a happiness and wellness that she had to go to the other side of the world to find within. Both Frances and Elizabeth find that by giving themselves permission to trust and follow their own deepest desires, they are able to create beautiful and fulfilling new lives. (Note: You don't have to be a world-traveling writer to tap into your own bulletproof spirit. Even if your only desire right now is leading you to a bowl of ice cream, revel in your own private little *dolce vita* and know that more will be revealed.)

Channeling Aladdin

Remember the story of Aladdin and his magic lamp? Kids from two to one hundred and two are enchanted by this story because it reveals a truth that we often forget, overlook, or begin to doubt: Aladdin reminds us that our wishes *will* be granted if we make it our business to *ask*. If you want to harness the power of your desires to help you manifest your dreams, you must channel your own inner Aladdin and begin to ask the universe to assist you. It doesn't matter what you call the creative and loving source of all that is—all that matters is that you actually *ask*. In the Gospel of Matthew, we are told "Ask, and it shall be given you; seek and ye shall find; knock and it shall be opened unto you" and this ancient truth about the connection between asking and receiving is found across cultures, religions, and centuries.

Spiritually fragile people are often uncomfortable asking for what they want. They feel that their desires somehow impose upon God or the universe, or they feel that they don't deserve what they desire. Spiritually bulletproof people understand that asking for what they want is a powerful way to begin to manifest their dreams. Resilient people know that the very act of asking sends a powerful signal inward to their own spirits and outward into a loving and abundant universe; they know that asking is actually a kind of deep humility and wisdom when it is accompanied by a genuine detachment from outcome. If you can know your own deepest desires and ask the universe to assist you in achieving them *without being attached to the outcome of your request,* you are onto something really big!

Dare to Detach

How do you develop a genuine attitude of detachment when you really, really, *really* want something to happen or work out a certain way? It may seem like detachment will only undermine your own best interests, but nothing could be further from the truth. When you're in the process of bouncing back, you're going to need to be able to allow your intense desire to fuel your thoughts, emotions, and actions so that they support the manifestation of your dreams. On the other hand, you will increase your resilience if you practice holding your desires lightly—try to cherish and nurture them without clinging to them or forcing them.

There's a verse from the Koran that really gets to the heart of what it means to cultivate an attitude of detachment: "Man should propose, only God can dispose." In a nutshell, you can want something all you want, but you must learn to open your heart to whatever outcome comes your way. Remember Frances and Elizabeth, our Italophile desire-following writer/heroines? Well, we won't ruin the books for you, but suffice it to say that, in the end, they both probably learn more about the art of detachment than the architecture of desire. The real lesson for them and for us is that when you learn to be detached from the outcome of your desires, all endings are happy endings.

When you are trying to bounce back from a hit, remember that you're really engaged in a dance of desire *and* detachment.

Also keep in mind how easy it is for these new dance partners to step on each other's toes. Detachment, more than desire, presents a huge challenge to us mere mortals, especially when we've been through the wringer and we just want something, *anything,* to go our way for once. You may find that it's very helpful to clarify what detachment *isn't:*

- Contrary to what many people believe, detachment is *not* forcing yourself to want nothing.
- An attitude of detachment is *not about* letting go of any goals and dreams you have and just drifting along aimlessly.
- Detachment is *not* a kind of spiritual apathy where you just don't care about anything all that much.

In truth, detachment is not really the *absence* of anything— it is the *presence* in your mind and heart of a willingness to place your personal desires within the context of the highest possible good. I'll give you two personal and concrete examples: As I sit here and write these words, I consciously balance my dreams for this book (*Millions of people come out on top of their heartbreaking hits! Oprah! New York Times bestseller!*) with praying that what I write ultimately accomplishes what God wants it to even if that means that my own plan goes out the window. In another chapter of my life, I was more interested in creating or nurturing another baby than another book. My passionate desire for a third child to complete our family was the creative energy that powered me through the labyrinthine and exhausting journey to my daughter. Without a doubt, I absolutely had to *really, really want* to do what I was doing—there was no room for apathy or disengagement. At the same time, I had to practice detachment on a minute-by-minute basis for almost four years as things unfolded in a far different manner than I had anticipated or planned. I had to free myself from attachments to *when* I'd have this baby and to what my baby might *be* like. I had to learn to become detached from any expectations about what the actual experience would be like and even from the certainty that my desire for a child would ultimately be fulfilled in any particular fashion at *all*. In the end, my desire did find fulfillment beyond my wildest dreams, but the journey to my child certainly did not unfold according to *my* original plan. I danced a dance of desire and detachment for more than a thousand days and nights and learned that this is the dance we must dance all our days if we want to be spiritually bulletproof.

When you dare to detach, you learn that you are not dancing alone—you are dancing with a universe that wants more for you than you could want for yourself and that is more abundant and brilliantly creative than you could ever imagine. In reality, your attachments to certain outcomes for your desires serve only to limit what's possible. The universe's plans for you, your dreams, and your life are larger and more miraculous than you would imagine for yourself, so dare to detach.

* * *

Bounce Back Boot Camp

Here are some ideas to help you get comfortable dancing between desire and detachment:

- Using your journal, begin to delve into your own desires. Put the heading WHAT I DESIRE at the top of the page and jot down anything that pops into your mind. Do not overthink this exercise or censor yourself in any way. You may find that you are very disconnected from your own desires and aren't sure what you want for yourself or your life. Or you may realize that you have been denying your deepest desires for years. Write down every desire you can think of, no matter how mundane or seemingly unrealistic. If you have no idea what to write, just jot down "I desire to discover my deepest desires." Just writing this list signals to your spirit that you're ready to begin to harness the power of your own desire to create the life of your dreams.

- Get in touch with your inner Aladdin. Begin to cultivate the art of asking. Start small so that you will be encouraged and emboldened by your success. Think of three little things that you desire and *ask* for them. Pay special attention to the nonmaterial desires that bubble up for you; maybe you'd really like it if your husband would rub your shoulders or maybe what you really desire is a little time alone once a week. Once you identify three small desires, ask for what you want. That may mean asking an actual person for a favor or some help, but it also may mean asking God or the universe to provide an opportunity or show you the way. When you ask, have every confidence that your desire will be fulfilled.

- Is there something that you really, really, *really* desire right now? Maybe you desperately want to reunite with your ex or maybe you are fixated on getting a promotion or having a baby. Perhaps you want to live abroad or simplify your life. At least once a day, exercise your detachment muscles by saying the following aloud:

*My desires are fully known and honored by Divine providence
and I feel safe in the knowledge that whatever the outcome,
the highest possible good flows easily and gracefully to me and through me.*

If you're pretty attached to your desires unfolding in a particular way, it might feel scary to turn them over so fully. You may feel some internal resistance as you say the words above. Remember that developing some detachment serves your own best interests, so allow yourself to let go a little.

•　•　•

Meet Your Meta-Consciousness

I am large, I contain multitudes.

—WALT WHITMAN

IN THE FIRST CHAPTER OF THIS BOOK, WE USED THE TERM "META-cognition" to describe the habit of "thinking about how you think." If you've tried using some of the techniques we suggest like thought-stopping or reframing, you were engaged in meta-cognition—you were literally *thinking about the way you think* and choosing to think about things in a way that best supports your resilience. Well, you've come a long way, baby, and now it's time to take this "meta" business to the next level. *Meta-consciousness* simply means "being conscious about your own consciousness." Consciousness is self-awareness, so raising your *meta-consciousness* means that you become more aware of your own self-awareness. Now, we know that all this "meta" stuff can be a little dizzying at first, but just bear with us for a bit and things will fall into place.

Spiritually bulletproof people have high levels of meta-consciousness that assist them in handling the hits that come their way. Resilient people consciously coordinate the different components of what they call the "self." They learn to differentiate the competing impulses or parts of themselves like ego, thought, and intuition, and are able to mediate and harmonize them. Though they experience internal conflicts like anyone else, spiritually bulletproof people are aware of and committed to coordinating the various parts of their "selves" so that they can respond most effectively to life's challenges.

Spiritually bulletproof people are aware of and committed to coordinating the various parts of their "selves" so that they can respond most effectively to life's challenges.

Developing and acting from this kind of meta-consciousness is one of the most important parts of their spiritual hygiene. When you develop and act from *your* meta-consciousness, you will tap into a well of spiritual resilience that will never run dry.

A House Divided

If you're like most people, you probably don't think of yourself as having lots of separate parts within what you call your "self." But as you look deeper, you'll discover that you really do contain many "sub-selves." When Martin Luther King, Jr., writes "Each of us is something of a schizophrenic personality, tragically divided against ourselves," he is touching upon one of the reasons why true spiritual resilience requires a certain degree of meta-consciousness; without some understanding of the different aspects of the self and the ability to coordinate them, it is much more difficult to handle life's heartbreaking hits. Abraham Lincoln's warning "A house divided against itself cannot stand" to a nation divided over the issue of slavery is still relevant to anyone facing adversity or crisis today. Your self is your "house," so to speak, and if the various parts of your self are not working well together, you *are* a "house divided" and you are, therefore, much easier to knock down and keep down.

A House with Many Rooms

Think of yourself as a really big house—a veritable mansion, a castle, even—with many rooms, some of which you have never explored and others you don't even know exist. Now imagine that the various rooms in the house symbolize parts of yourself such as your survival instinct, desire, emotion, thought, and intuition. When you're in each of these rooms, you can only act based on the information that particular room offers you. For example, when you're in your "emotion room," you cannot use logic at all. Can you see that it might be better to call your boss from one room and fight off an attacker in another? Can you see how limiting it would be if you hung out in only a few rooms of your house when you had so many to choose from? What if there were whole areas of your house that you had never even discovered? Have you ever had a dream where you found yourself wandering in a part of your house that you never even knew was there? This dream is a very common one and often signals the development of a new self-awareness or mastery over an aspect of the self. Raising your meta-consciousness is like exploring all the nooks and crannies of your house and then installing an intercom system so that all the rooms can communicate.

We Could Make Beautiful Music Together

Let's try another metaphor. Imagine a symphony orchestra. The various subparts of your self are the musicians. Maybe your ego plays the cello and your survival instinct is on drums. Picture your imagination playing the flute and your logical thought playing the clarinet. Without a conductor, it would be pretty hard for the different musicians to coordinate themselves. Your self is the conductor directing the orchestra, cueing in the brass and percussion sections as needed. The more developed your meta-consciousness, the more skilled you'll be at conducting. Now, let's extend this metaphor. If what you'd call your "self" is conducting, who has composed the music that you're using? Imagine that the composer is your "Higher Self"—the part of you that is always in contact with and has full access to universal wisdom and grace. Think about how helpful it would be for you to be able to consult the composer when you had questions or problems conducting a new piece of music. When you develop your meta-consciousness, you get the composer, the conductor, and all the musicians in one place, and with your combined resources, you are able to make beautiful music.

Me, Myself, and I

The ancient Taoist proverb "He who knows others is learned; he who knows himself is wise" points to the value of getting more meta-conscious. If you want to connect with your bulletproof spirit, you cannot just "pass by" your self anymore. You must take the journey inward. When you do, you'll find that what you call your "self" is an incredibly complex constellation of qualities, beliefs, primal instincts, thoughts, emotions, impulses, drives, and intuitive faculties. There are many schools of psychology and philosophy devoted to mapping that constellation and navigating it, but the self is so vast and complex, no map can ever really capture it. For our purposes, let's keep things very simple and just focus on three parts of the self. Being able to mediate and synergize the energies of these three parts of yourself will dramatically increase your spiritual resilience.

The Survivor Self

The ancient Greek aphorism *Know Thyself* was inscribed at the Temple of Apollo in Delphi and has challenged philosophers and thinkers ever since. Maybe you're not sure you really *want* to know yourself—perhaps you feel like Germany's man of letters, Johann Wolfgang von Goethe, did about the whole thing: "Know thyself? If I knew myself, I'd run away." Maybe you're afraid of what you'll find if you look too deep below the surface; as Fyodor Dostoyevsky writes "There are . . . things which a man is afraid to tell even to himself, and every decent man has a number of such things stored away in his mind." Well, all of the things that you are afraid to tell even yourself are hanging out together in a part of yourself that we'll call the *Survivor Self.*

Have you ever seen the reality TV show *Survivor*? On this show, the contestants all vie for a big cash prize by doing whatever it takes to "out-survive" each other in an inhospitable environment with limited resources. Each *Survivor* contestant is there to win—to take home the prize—no matter what they have to do to win it. Your Survivor Self sees life as a big contest where there can be only one winner and where there's not nearly enough to go around. This part of your self doesn't necessarily care if you are happy, peaceful, or emotionally stable—it just wants you to either live or win!

Many of your Survivor Self's motivations and influences are hidden from your conscious mind, but it always gets involved when you have taken a hit. Your Survivor Self has a very important role to play in helping you deal with adversity and crisis, but many times it tries to run the entire show, and this is what can cause lots of problems for you if you're trying to bounce back from a tough hit. Your Survivor Self has a very distinctive voice that you will be able to recognize once you start paying attention. When you've taken a serious hit, these are the types of things you might hear it saying:

- *You can't let them get away with this! Someone's gotta pay!*
- *You must never, ever forgive him for what he's done.*
- *If you don't watch out, you are going to wind up on the street like a bag lady.*
- *You're going to go through all these hellish treatments and then just end up dying anyway.*
- *You deserve what you got—it's your own fault! You better make sure that doesn't happen again!*
- *Leave her before she leaves you—at least you'll have your pride.*
- *See, now you're all alone, just like I told you you'd be.*

As you've probably already figured out, your Survivor Self comes from a place of fear. This fear walks around wearing a lot of costumes—it can look like anger, vengeance, insecurity, hopelessness, defensiveness, pride, and resignation—but under all the masks, it's just plain fear. Now, before you get too down on this part of your self, remember that your Survivor Self is just doing its job—it is trying to help you survive by keeping you on your toes, vigilant to anything that might harm you. But what happens is that your Survivor Self has a very loud and assertive voice and wants to get involved and run the show, especially when you're in crisis or have taken a hit. It drowns out the voices of the other parts of your self, and sometimes, it's the voice we've mistakenly learned to rely on the most for guidance and direction. In order to develop more spiritual resilience, you'll need to train your Survivor Self to be more of a team player. Let's take a peek at the rest of the team.

The Sacred Self

If you're like most people, you are quite familiar with the voice of your Survivor Self—maybe because it pipes up all the time or because it speaks so loudly. You may not have had the pleasure of making the acquaintance of what we'll call your *Sacred Self* even though it has always been there, waiting for you to say hello.

Your Sacred Self is like a wise grandmother or grandfather who sits and waits for you to come listen to some wise counsel. Your Sacred Self is always sitting patiently and quietly within you, watching over you and silently witnessing all that happens to you. This part of your self has all the answers you'll ever need and all the love you'd ever want and it has all the time in the world for you and your problems. This Sacred Self is the part of your self that has a direct and open line to universal wisdom and grace and is dedicated to your genuine happiness, peace, and spiritual evolution. It is also available to console, comfort, and counsel you whenever and wherever you need assistance.

Not relying on your Sacred Self when you're having a hard time is like having a cardiologist in the apartment next door and not feeling comfortable enough to knock on the door when you're having chest pains in the middle of the night. You need to get better acquainted with your Sacred Self so that you can start benefiting from this amazing resource. Since this part of your self often speaks softly or waits to be consulted, you may not be that familiar with its voice. Here are some things your Sacred Self might say when you are struggling or have taken a serious hit:

- *There were victims at both ends of the gun.*
- *If you forgive her, you'll free yourself from more suffering.*
- *You will always have all you need. You are safe.*
- *You are in the process of healing right now and all will be well.*
- *Everyone makes mistakes. What amazing lessons you're learning.*
- *Take a chance—keep your heart open.*
- *You are never alone—you are connected to others at the level of your spirit.*

When, an hour and a half after learning that his son had been murdered, Azim received a "message" from his spirit that told him that there were victims on both ends of the gun that took his son's life, he was able to receive the wisdom and grace of his Sacred Self. As you can see, the Sacred Self comes from a place of total love. It also likes to play dress-up, so it can show up as feelings of compassion, forgiveness, abundance, faith, gratitude, vulnerability, or unity. This part of your self really deserves your attention because it always steers you in the direction of your highest good. Just like your Survivor Self needs to learn to be a better team player, your Sacred Self needs to step up to the plate and take on a larger role in managing the team.

The Synergizing Self

Synergy means that the whole is greater than the sum of its parts. The opposite of synergy is antagonism, which refers to the whole being less than the sum of its parts. If you have a low level of meta-consciousness, the different parts that comprise the self end up acting in antagonistic ways—and as we've already established, a house divided against itself cannot stand up to the hits that come its way. Fortunately, the Survivor Self and the Sacred Self have a third partner to help them work together—the *Synergizing Self.* This part of your self is much more available to your conscious awareness than are the other two parts. The Synergizing Self is the part of you that can consciously work to raise awareness of the other parts of the self and then mediate and harmonize their contributions. This part of your self can act like the conductor of the symphony to create something beautiful out of chaos. The Synergizing Self has its own way of responding when you've taken a bullet. Here are some things it might say:

- *I know that your first instinct is to lash out—it's only human to feel that way. Take a deep breath and count to ten. There's got to be a better way to see this, one that will bring you peace.*
- *What happened to you cannot be condoned—there need to be consequences so it never happens again. When you forgive, you're not letting the other guy off the hook as much as you're letting yourself off the hook.*

- *It's clear that you need to make better financial decisions in the future but it will work out; all you need will come your way if you open yourself up to new opportunities.*
- *It's natural to have some anxiety about these medical procedures or treatments, but you will respond to them and heal.*
- *You probably now realize that you really didn't handle that situation very well. You've learned a lot from your mistake and are committed to a positive outcome.*
- *You need to establish clear boundaries and expectations with this person, but you also are willing to keep your heart open and try again.*
- *You need to take responsibility for making authentic connections with other people, but remember, you're never really alone when you're connected to your spiritual source.*

Your Synergizing Self is able to assist you through adversity by integrating the protective elements of your Survivor Self and the nurturing, visionary elements of your Sacred Self. Your Synergizing Self allows you to tap into and listen to the many aspects of your self so that you achieve an effect that is greater than the sum of its parts. This Synergizing Self relies on instinct, intellect, and intuition equally and also grows in effectiveness when you become conscious of its presence. Though it's not always easy when things get challenging, try to isolate the voices of your different selves and listen to them with greater attention. You will be amazed at the inner resources available to you when you meet your meta-consciousness!

• • •

Bounce Back Boot Camp

Here are some ideas to help you raise your meta-consciousness:

- When you're in reaction mode, it is likely that you're unconsciously responding to the shrill voice of your Survivor

Self. When you find yourself feeling highly reactive to a person or situation, try to pause and reflect upon this new awareness. It's as simple as taking a deep breath and saying "Okay, all of these feelings and reactions are coming from my Survivor Self and this is only one voice that I should pay attention to. I am taking note of this voice's concerns, but I am going to check in with my other selves, too." Like all thinking habits, this one will feel stilted or forced at first but will eventually become second nature.

- Consulting with your Sacred Self is a critical part of good spiritual hygiene. Some people meditate on a particular question, trusting that they will find an answer in the stillness. Others use active prayer, asking God or the universe to guide them or reveal something that's needed. Often, your Sacred Self will try to make itself heard through your intuition. Paying attention to flashes of insight or "hunches" is helpful. When you just "know" something in your heart or your gut, recognize that your Sacred Self speaks through this intuition. Actually *asking* for assistance is very important—when you ask, it will answer.

- When you are dealing with a crisis or have taken a hit, actually plan a little meeting where you can get your three "selves" together to strategize. Check in with each "self." Your Survivor Self will usually want to "speak" first and will come out in your initial reactions to or feelings about what's going on. Your Sacred Self may need to be "consulted." Let your Synergizing Self take notes on what is "said" and come up with a list of next steps to take. These meetings will make you feel silly when you first start having them, but as your meta-consciousness increases, they will happen spontaneously and proceed more quickly and gracefully. You'll be amazed at how much more resilient you'll be when you're tapping into all of the resources at your disposal.

• • •

SECRET #21

Be Present to the Present

Trying to understand is like straining through muddy water.
Be still and allow the mud to settle.

—LAO-TZU

SPIRITUALLY FRAGILE PEOPLE FEEL TERRIBLY OUT OF CONTROL WHEN they cannot know the outcome of a situation they're facing or when they can't find answers immediately. They also spend a lot of their time and energy focusing on what happened in the past or worrying about what will happen in the future. Spiritually bulletproof people ride the waves of adversity with more ease and grace because they believe that the answers they seek will be revealed in perfect time and in the perfect way. They learn to be in the void of "not-knowing" without losing their minds or their faith and they also learn to live fully in the present moment.

If you're like most people, you may spend shockingly little time being "present to the present." It's really easy to take the present moment completely for granted and spend all your time revisiting the past and planning a future that hasn't yet arrived.

Calvin and Hobbes cartoonist Bill Watterson believes that "Often it takes some calamity to make us live in the present." Merriam-Webster's dictionary defines calamity as "a state of deep distress or misery caused by major misfortune or loss," and when you've taken a serious hit, you are definitely in this state! Since calamity really can propel you into a higher level of being present to the present, it serves you in a very profound way. When calamity strikes and you are in no-man's land, where no solutions or answers are clear, the universe is giving you a chance to sign up for your own personal tutorial in learning to live in the present moment.

Spiritually bulletproof people are committed to living in the present moment, releasing the past and letting the future unfold in its own way and at its own pace.

Though it is not always easy, spiritually bulletproof people are committed to living in the present moment, releasing the past and letting the future unfold in its own way and at its own pace.

While there *are* a few people out there who naturally and entirely inhabit the present moment and who are completely comfortable in the void of not knowing how things will turn out, most spiritually bulletproof people must choose to *learn* this new way of being and must commit to practicing some habits that support it. If you want to give your resilience a huge boost, begin to practice a kind of "time management" where you consciously choose the present as your preferred hangout. Since the most manageable way to get through any crisis is to take it moment by moment, learning this new kind of time management is one of the best, most loving things you can do for yourself.

The Ultimate Present

The richness and sweetness of life exist only in the present moment. The past and the future are not alive to you, and can never offer you the joy your heart desires. It is often said that the present is a gift—can you see that it's really a *present* that waits for you to open it and experience it? If you can give yourself the *present* of being fully *present* to the *present,* you will transform your life in a very real and practical way. (Let this triple *present* become your new mantra.)

If you're dealing with loss or crisis, learning to really live in the present moment will provide you with a practical way to find relief from your heartache or pain. This is not some silly, outlandish idea; it is a really useful and concrete thing you can do for yourself to help you handle the hits that come your way. As Irish poet Oliver Goldsmith writes "A great source of calamity lies in regret and anticipation; therefore a person is wise who thinks of the present alone, regardless of the past or future." If you can train your mind to resist the backward pull of the past and to avoid the obsessive hamster wheel of future-focused thinking, you will find yourself hanging out in the present moment. And you will quickly discover that hits are a lot easier to handle from there.

All Not Present, Raise Your Hands

If you've taken a serious hit, you may find it next to impossible to keep your mind away from the past and the future. Take a look at the list below and see if you are checking out of the present moment a bit too often:

- You find yourself mentally rehashing certain conversations or conflicts.
- You analyze situations from the past over and over again, trying to figure out what went wrong or trying to understand what really happened.
- You keep hearing someone's comments or accusations in your mind. You cannot get what was said out of your head.

- You often think of something that you regret having done or not having done.
- You replay certain scenes in your head. You visualize scenarios from the past that cause you pain or sadness.
- You wish you could go back in time and change something you did or didn't do.
- You feel a lot of anxiety about the future and spend a lot of time trying to figure out what it will bring your way.
- You obsess over the details of future plans and go over and over them in your mind.
- You have a hard time sleeping because you can't stop thinking about all the things you need to do.
- You can't relax because you need to know how a particular situation will turn out.
- You fantasize a lot about the future.
- You think that you'll be a lot happier in the future, when things are different.

Don't worry if you recognize yourself in some of these statements—almost everyone does! And, of course, it's only natural to spend some time thinking about the past and the future; it's important to learn from mistakes and plan for the future and it's also fun to reminisce and fantasize. But without a conscious commitment to living in the present, you may be spending all of your time living in places that aren't even real and missing out on the moments that really matter. If you want to make the present your default setting, start by limiting the time you spend in the past and in the future.

Years ago, after a profound conversation with the Dalai Lama, Azim decided that he wanted to become more "present to the present," so he started a journal where he kept track of every time he thought about the past or the future. He wanted to know where he was spending all of his "mental time." He discovered that he spent almost no time thinking about the past but that he was *constantly* thinking about the future. He realized that all he had to do to live more fully in the present moment was stop visiting the future so much. He used "thought-stopping" to break his habit of spinning out of the present into the future. Every time he found himself "in the future," he brought himself back to the present moment by focusing on his body and his breathing. He felt his feet on the ground and became aware of the breath entering and leaving his body. He trained himself away from the future and found that he was much happier and more effective when he was spending more of his time in the present.

If you track your own thoughts, you'll begin to notice where your mind likes to hang out. This simple awareness can really help you to inhabit the present moment. Like all habits of the mind, this one gets easier and more natural with practice. If you want to be more "present to the present," stop hanging out in the past or the future. Staying in the present moment may not be *easy* at first, but it really is that *simple*.

On a "Need-to-Know" Basis

If you want to come out on top of the hits you take, one of the most essential things you must learn to do is to let go of your "need to know." Crises, losses, and disappointments tend to make a mess of things in our lives and disrupt our plans. Very often, they leave us openmouthed and staring out into an uncertain future. Spiritually fragile people are often tortured by their "need to know" how things will turn out. This desire to know the outcome up front is very common and natural, but it also sets us up for great anxiety, since life doesn't like to ruin the ending by telling us up front how it will all go down. A big part of handling the hits that come your way and coming out on top of them has to do with how well you are able to manage your mind while waiting for the clarity that eventually follows any calamity. Unfortunately—or perhaps fortunately—you will spend much of your life in a state of "not-knowing"; you may need to find a way to live for days, weeks, months, or even years in this void. Spiritually bulletproof people realize this truth about life and cultivate a willingness to live with joy within the void of not-knowing. Letting go of your "need to know" is easier when you keep yourself "present to the present." When you're able to do both of these things, you will send your resilience through the roof.

Real-Life Graduate School

Learning to live in the void of not-knowing is part of spiritual maturation. One of the greatest teachers for learning to live in the present and letting go of our "need to know" often comes dressed up like illness or disease. If life is spiritual school, there's no doubt that, in general, the classes get more challenging the longer you stay on campus. No one willingly signs up for "Heart Disease 101" or "Parkinson's Seminar" or "Advanced Breast Cancer," but if you find yourself sitting in one of these courses, you are being given the chance to learn things that your spirit is ready to take on. You will never be enrolled in a class that you don't have the aptitude to handle, so take some pride in the fact that you're in an upper-level course! I'd like to introduce you to two real-life "honor students" in the school of life, who live in the void of not-knowing. Meet my friend Mike:

> Mike owns the service station in the small town where I live. He is in his late fifties and has the energy of a thirty-year-old. He was diagnosed last year with end-stage coronary artery and peripheral vascular disease, and his doctors tell him that he has between two and five years to live. They've told him to visit the people he needs to visit and get all of his affairs—business and personal—in order. His arteries and veins are failing him faster than the doctors can fix them through bypass procedures and other treatments. The best he can hope for is to aggressively manage blockages and aneurysms with medication and through sur-

geries; he is already covered from ankles to groin to neck with angry red scars that hurt and heal poorly because of his circulation difficulties. He knows that he could suffer a fatal embolism or aneurysm at any time; Mike tells me that he is a "walking time bomb." The amazing thing is, he tells me all this with a huge smile on his face after filling my tank with gas while standing in the twenty-degree weather two days after leaving the hospital for his fourth surgery this year. When I ask Mike how he maintains such a positive attitude in the face of such uncertainty, he reminds me that, truth be told, we're all really walking time bombs—he's just more acutely aware than most people are of how fragile and precious each day is. He also tells me that he avoids thinking about the pain of his past surgeries and refuses to obsess about the future and what it may hold for him. He focuses, instead, on each moment and the joy it contains. In many ways, Mike is more alive now than he has ever been before. He finds that there is nothing to be unhappy about in the present moment, so that is where he keeps his attention. He is not in denial about the reality of his situation—he is just choosing to live with joy within the void of not-knowing. His ability to stay in the present moment allows him to be truly happy. He tells me that the trick is to live this way every day.

Now, let me introduce you to another great soul:

Frank is the chair of the English Department at the college where I teach. He's also a dear friend. Two years ago, Frank was diagnosed with Parkinson's disease—he was 59 years old. He is a very handsome, athletic man who runs marathons, and he runs circles around his younger colleagues. His boyish looks and agility seem completely at odds with the new reality he now confronts. When he tells me of his diagnosis, he comforts me when I cry. I really loved Frank before the Parkinson's, but now I am blown away by his bulletproof spirit. A few years into this new reality, he can no longer easily run his beloved road races and his hands shake when he lectures. Typing has become problematic for this award-winning writer and speaking in front of audiences has become stressful. Frank is losing so many little things that are dear to his heart and wrapped up with his personal and professional identity, and when he looks down the road, he knows that there are more losses ahead of him. When I ask him how he maintains such a good attitude, he tells me that he is glad for the chance to approach this thing—this disease—with the same game attitude he's brought to all the challenges he's faced in his life. As someone who's done well at everything he's tried his hand at, Frank sees this as an opportunity to inspire the people he meets with his willingness to do this well, too. He also tells me "Today is a good day. Everything is good today," and his focus on the present moment is one of his ways of doing this well. Frank is a brilliant man and he keeps up with the medical literature and research that may offer him hope for treatment or, one day, a cure. But he doesn't spend time worrying about the worst-case scenarios that he may face in the future. He is taking this journey one day at a time, focusing on what he can do, not on what he has lost. In a distinguished thirty-five-year career in academia, it's clear that he's doing some of his very finest teaching now by showing his family, friends, colleagues, and students how to take a hit and come out on top. He understands that "coming out on top" may have more to do with how he lives with his disease than it does with beating it.

If, like Mike, you knew that your days were numbered, would you choose to be more present to each moment of the present? If, like Frank, your future was filled with uncertainty, would you waste your precious time nursing wounds from the past or obsessing over the future? Take a minute to pause right now and think about this present moment:

Feel your feet on the ground. Notice the air coming in through your nose and mouth and filling up your lungs. Become aware of the clothing that surrounds your body and brushes against your skin. Feel the temperature of the air around you and notice the light that fills the space you're in. Listen to what you hear all around you. Is there a fan blowing or a furnace humming? Become aware of the position of your body and notice how it is supported by furniture or just by gravity. Pay attention to what your eyes can take in as they move around the room and notice what it feels like to move your eyes so fluidly. Again, become aware of your breath and thank the universe for supporting you so effortlessly and lovingly with the oxygen that feeds your cells. Finally, feel your feet on the ground again and thank the universe for effortlessly and lovingly supporting you in all you do.

Were you able to become a little more present to the present moment? If you were, did you notice how you lost track of time, and how any worries or concerns on your mind seemed to vanish? Can you imagine feeling like this more every day? Would you believe me if I told you that there are some people who walk around all day, every day, totally present to each moment? Would you like to give yourself some more of this gift? Can you see that the past and the future are only shadows and shimmering reflections of the present and that to spend all your time there is to be half alive? Do you understand that when you're in the past or the future, you dream and are, therefore, asleep to the present? What if I reminded you that, just like Mike, your days *are* numbered? What if I reminded you that, just like Frank, your future *is* uncertain? Would you want to spend your time here so thoughtlessly, so foolishly? Will it take a calamity for you to notice that the present really *is* a present—all wrapped up with a shiny ribbon—for you to open every day?

Learning how to live in peace within the void of not-knowing takes time and practice, and learning how to stay in the present moment is a major spiritual accomplishment. Life asks so much of us, but it also gives us so many chances to grow into the selves we'll need to be to handle the hits that come our way. Begin to see the hits you take as opportunities to become more resilient. Your bulletproof spirit lives in the eternal present and is waiting to assist you through any and all adversity—ask it to take the lead as you deal with the hits that come your way.

• • •

Bounce Back Boot Camp

Try out some of these techniques to help you become more "present to the present":

- When your world has been rocked by a serious blow, it is natural to have moments when you feel panicked about the future. These are the times when you need to remind yourself to release your "need to know." Post the following prayer where you'll see it and pause to read it throughout the day:

  I live in a universe that manages the rotation of the earth and its journey around the sun. I believe that this universe can manage my problems and my journey through life. I release my need to know now and open my heart to the peace that comes from trusting that everything is unfolding as it should.

- Use your journal to keep track of where your mind tends to hang out. Do you frequently find yourself in the past or are you visiting the future a little too often? Try to monitor your mind for a mere five minutes. Use two columns— one marked PAST and the other marked FUTURE—and keep a tally of how many times you find your mind spiraling backward into the past or spinning forward into the future. You'll be amazed at how little you are able to remain in the present moment even when you are conscious about what you're doing. You may find that you are able to stay in the present for less than one minute out of the five you are devoting to this exercise. Just like keeping a journal of all your expenditures will help you figure out where all your money is going, doing this exercise will help you see where all your attention is going. The good news is that, with practice, you can actually train your mind to stay in the present most of the time. And once you get a taste for the bliss of the present moment, you'll never want to leave.

- One powerful way to not "be" in the past is to do the healing work necessary so that you can forgive what happened in the past. Strengthening your forgiveness practice will profoundly impact your ability to stay more present to the present.

- In order to become more present to the present moment, you must practice keeping your awareness in the present moment. Think about the tiny little meditation exercise we tried in this chapter. Imagine expanding that moment of greater awareness into extended periods. Make the decision to learn and practice the art of meditation or centering prayer. You don't need to devote hours a day to meditation for it to help you. In fact, if you meditate for three to five minutes a day, you will begin to see benefits. We can't teach you how to meditate in one little chapter here, but we can promise you that when you take the initiative to begin a small meditation practice, you will be rewarded with ever-increasing levels of spiritual resilience. Jack Kornfield's book *Meditation for Beginners* is one of many excellent guides to help get you started. You can also visit our website for more information and links to some helpful sites.

• • •

Banish Busyness

It is not enough to be busy; so are the ants.
The question is: what are we busy about?

—Henry David Thoreau

When you've taken a serious hit and are trying to come out on top of it, it's important to do all you can to speed yourself along. Sometimes that means *adding* certain things to your life— like meditating or creating a sacred space in which to heal. But other times, the best way to assist yourself is to actually *eliminate* things that diminish your ability to bounce back. One of the most powerful things you can do to turbo-charge your resilience is to banish busyness from your life.

Spiritually fragile people often mistake being busy with having a full life or being successful, but the feeling of being too busy all of the time can also stem from an unacknowledged sense that they're wasting their lives. Spiritually bulletproof people know that busyness is not enough—they ask themselves, as Thoreau did, "What are we busy about?" While their lives are filled with family, friends, meaningful work, and recreation, spiritually bulletproof people banish *busyness* from their lives to make room for the real *business* of living an authentic, intentional life.

> Spiritually bulletproof people banish *busyness* from their lives to make room for the real *business* of living an authentic, intentional life.

This is no time for you to be running around like a chicken with its head cut off. It is really hard to avoid the manic busyness that has consumed our society, but when you're dealing with a difficult blow or struggling through adversity, it's vital that you cut out the extra nonsense. You need to pay attention to the fact that the universe has just placed an enormous speed bump in your path—perhaps it's trying to tell you something. Maybe comedian Steven Wright is on to something when he says "I think God's going to come down and pull civilization over for speeding." If you've taken a heartbreaking hit, you're probably a little shaky behind the wheel right now anyway—this is certainly no time to drive fast. When you make the decision to banish *busyness* from your life, you begin to reclaim the time and space to engage in the real *business* of your life—the things you came here to do.

Busy Being Born

You may be saying to yourself "What's the big deal about being busy? I mean, all the stuff I'm doing is good stuff and, anyway, it doesn't help to complain about it because I have to do it." This chapter is absolutely *not* about dropping all of the people, things, and activities that give your life joy and meaning. We are *not* suggesting that you sit around doing nothing all the time. What we *are* asking you to do is to pay more attention to how well the *busyness* of your life is supporting the real *business* you came to this planet to take care of. When in his song "It's Alright, Ma (I'm Only

Bleeding)" Bob Dylan warns us that "he not busy being born is busy dying," he reveals one of the biggest reasons that busyness is bad for us—it prevents us from becoming all we're meant to be in this life by keeping us all wrapped up in other things that have nothing at all to do with our true destinies. If you're "busy being born," you have the freedom to spend some of your emotional energy and actual time on the process of becoming your authentic self. When you are so busy every day that you neglect your own spiritual journey and development, you really are "busy dying."

Alan Lakein is an expert on personal time management and the author of *How to Get Control of Your Time and Your Life*. He believes that "Time is equal to life; therefore, waste your time and waste your life, or master your time and master your life." Banishing busyness is the beginning of mastering both your time and your life. It can also be the beginning of remembering who you really are. Jack Kornfield, who trained as a Buddhist monk and is one of the foremost meditation teachers in the West, reminds us that "When we get too caught up in the busyness of the world we lose connection with one another—and ourselves." When you banish busyness, you begin to reestablish and strengthen your connection with yourself. Being really, really busy can keep you in a very mechanical mode of living. Psychologist Erich Fromm predicted our modern predicament almost a century ago when he pointed out that "The danger of the past was that men became slaves. The danger of the future is that man may become robots." If you find yourself feeling numb or depressed, busyness may be robbing you of your vitality. Consider what French writer Octave Mirbeau had to say about busyness:

> You're obliged to pretend respect for people and institutions you think absurd. You live attached in a cowardly fashion to moral and social conventions you despise, condemn, and know lack all foundation.

Obviously, Octave is pretty down on busyness, but he makes some valid points. What distinguishes *busyness* from the real *busi-*

ness that deserves your time and energy is intentionality and authenticity. If your days and years are filled with a lot of stuff that you wouldn't really choose to do if you had your own way, then your busyness is a *major* problem. And if your agenda is jam-packed with people, places, and activities that don't feed your soul or speak to "the real you," then something's gotta give. When you've taken a serious hit and are working to come out on top of it, it is *especially* important that your days and life are filled with relationships and activities that you've *chosen* and that reflect and nurture your *authentic* self. Banishing busyness is all about clearing the decks so that this is possible.

A Busy Quizzy

If you're like most people, you probably don't even realize how much of your time is squandered by busyness. This little "Busyness Quiz" may bring things into focus for you. Put a little check next to each statement that rings true for you.

❏ My days seem to blend together and go by in a blur.

❏ Most of my day is spent doing things that I feel I have to do, not that I really want to do.

❏ I spend a lot of time talking with people about stuff I'm not really all that interested in.

❏ I spend most of my time with people I'm thrown together with by work, family obligations, or my children's activities. I don't have much time to spend with my closest friends.

❏ My To-Do list is filled with endless drudgery, and no matter how much I accomplish, it just seems to get longer and longer.

❏ Lately, I feel like going to church or religious services is more of a chore than anything else. It doesn't really "fill me up," but I feel obligated to attend.

❏ One or more of the organizations I belong to doesn't really interest me anymore, but I stay involved out of habit or a sense of duty.

❏ I feel pressured by other people to participate in certain activities. Secretly, I wish I could just bail out.

❏ I feel pressure to "make an appearance" at certain social functions, even though I really don't enjoy myself when I attend.

❏ I spend money on things I don't really want or can't afford because I feel that I must conform to others' expectations. For example, I always feel obligated to attend and buy something when I'm invited to a Tupperware, basket, craft, or jewelry party.

❏ I wish I could change my life, but a lot of people depend on me to keep doing everything I currently do.

❏ I push my children to participate in sports, clubs, or other activities because I'm worried that they'll be at a disadvantage if they don't.

❏ I spend a lot of time cleaning and maintaining my home. I think that other people will think less of me if I don't keep up appearances.

❏ I'm not fulfilled in my job but it pays the bills.

❏ I live for the weekend, but when it arrives, I have so many chores to do that I can't even really enjoy it.

❏ I feel like a robot, just going through the same drill day after day.

If you checked more than three statements, it's definitely time to banish some of the busyness that's keeping you from the real business you're meant to take care of while you're here in this precious life. The first step is to acknowledge that busyness is preventing you from living a more intentional and authentic life.

A Tale of Two Rabbits

If you try to do everything you're "supposed" to do or that society "expects" you to do, you will not have enough time to do what your soul came here to do. Like the old Chinese proverb cautions "If you chase two rabbits, you will lose them both." If you want to tap into the full power of your bulletproof spirit, you must let go of the illusion that you can successfully chase two rabbits. When you've taken a hit, you find yourself in a defining moment of your life. You have been brought to a crossroads; you can choose a new direction. Making an inspired choice at this defining moment can make all the difference in whether or not you come out on top of your hit. As you begin to rebuild your life, getting back on the treadmill of *busyness* is the path of least resistance. But you *must* resist this path because it's not even a *path*— it's just a *treadmill* that gives you the illusion of forward motion.

* * *

Bounce Back Boot Camp

Here are some things to consider as you begin to banish the busyness from your life:

- First of all, remind yourself that no one has a gun to your head. You have the freedom to make choices about how you spend your precious time, but you must give yourself permission to exercise this freedom. You *can* change things if you really want to and if you're willing to push through some initial discomfort.

- Letting go of your need for other people's approval is absolutely essential. If you're honest with yourself, you'll realize that a great deal of your busyness is caused by your fear of what other people will think or say if you change the way you spend your time. For example, you may stay involved in the PTA more out of worry over what the other moms will think of you than out of any genuine belief that you are really helping make your kids' schools better. Rather than attend meetings because you're afraid not to, consider helping out in a way that you choose to and that is more authentic for you.

- If guilt gets in the way of you banishing busyness, remind yourself that what you *should* feel guilty about is neglecting the real business of authentic living. When you're so busy doing stuff you don't really want to be doing that you don't have any time to do the things you really want to do, you are cheating the universe out of the contributions that only the "real you" can make. (Read that last sentence a second time and let it sink in.)

- If you are just "going through the motions" with your religious routines, it's time to get real. There is nothing more deadening to the soul than a mechanical approach to spirituality. Getting on an authentic spiritual path is arguably the most important task of adult life—begin today to invest some time and energy in finding a path with a heart. If you need to drop something else in your life to make time for a spiritual practice that really feeds your soul, then do it— it will be one of the best decisions you ever make. Visit our website for ideas to help you get started.

- You may need to break your busyness addiction by going cold turkey. Consider doing nothing for an entire week or even a month just to see what you miss and what you can happily live without. Put a moratorium on extracurricular activities for whatever period of time you decide upon. Tell your friends, family, and colleagues that you're taking a "busyness break" and then just say no to *everything*. During this time, do only those things that you literally *must* do—work, essential chores, sacred obligations. If you're like most people, you've probably been using busyness to avoid the business of authentic living and, if that's the case, you may feel very uncomfortable having so much free time. At first, you may have no idea how you really want to fill your time, but if you're patient, clues about the real business you're here to accomplish will surface. On the other hand, you may have known all along what you really want to do with your time but have never given yourself the space to actually do it. Whatever is going on for you, use your journal to process your feelings.

● ● ●

SECRET #23

Reconsider Consistency

Consistency is the last refuge of the unimaginative. .

—OSCAR WILDE

WE'VE BEEN REMINDING YOU SINCE THE VERY FIRST CHAPTER OF THIS book that you don't need to *become* spiritually bulletproof because you already *are* spiritually bulletproof. Your journey is one of remembering and choosing to honor the truth about yourself. It's also a process of stripping away anything that stands between you and your bulletproof spirit—peeling away layers that do not serve you or your resilience. In the last chapter, we urged you to begin to banish the busyness that stands in the way of you taking care of the real business of authentic living. This chapter invites you to continue the clean sweep you've started so that you can get closer to the full power of your bulletproof spirit. Next in line for the recycling bin: your unconscious attachment to consistency—a sneaky little nonvirtue that can control a lot more of your life than you might imagine possible.

What is consistency? You might be thinking "Isn't consistency a good thing? Don't kids need consistency in their routines and in the way we discipline them?" And you're right, consistency *can* be beneficial—if you're trying to get your child's napping routine squared away. When Ralph Waldo Emerson writes that "A foolish consistency is the hobgoblin of little minds," he refers to the kind of consistency that we're concerned with here—an unthinking attachment to the status quo. Oliver Wendell Holmes, Jr., gets to the core of consistency's corrupting influence upon us when he writes "Most of the things we do, we do for no better reason than that our fathers have done them or that our neighbors do them, and the same is true of a larger part than we suspect of what we think."

> Spiritually bulletproof people reject the idea that there's any "one way" to do things and are willing to depart from tradition, habit, or custom in order to create a more authentic life for themselves.

When you do things the way they've "always been done" or when you stick with the status quo, you may feel safe because you're "playing by the rules," but, as Katharine Hepburn famously cautioned "If you obey all the rules you miss all the fun." If you want to turbo-charge your resilience, start questioning all of the "rules" that are running your life. Spiritually hearty people are comfortable questioning authority and rejecting the status quo. While they are not by any means "rebels without a cause," spiritually bulletproof people reject the idea that there's any "one way" to do things and are willing to depart from tradition, habit, or custom in order to create a more authentic life for themselves.

It's important to note that spiritually resilient people are absolutely not trying to be different just for the *sake* of being different—it's just that they are highly conscious about the choices they make and the influences they consider as they make those choices. On the other hand, spiritually fragile people tend to stick with the status quo and cling to consistency, though they are often quite unaware of this fact. This fear of change often prevents them from "rising from the ashes" after they've been burned by life's trials. If you've taken a major blow and are going to bother rebuilding your life, you may as well build an authentic one—this is no time to stick with the status quo just because it's what you've always known. Now is the time to reconsider consistency and create a life that reflects the real you. If you do this, then the hits you've taken won't have been in vain.

Sink or Swim

When you're in the middle of a crisis, it can feel like the ship you've been sailing has sunk and you're lost at sea without a lifeboat. When you're trying to keep yourself afloat, the last thing you need is lots of extra weight dragging you down. When you walk through life thinking that there's only one way to do things, it's like you're floundering in the ocean wearing a suit of armor or a giant ball gown with sixty pounds of sequins sewn on. If you want to survive and swim to land, you've got to strip away what's pulling you down.

Grace Hopper certainly had her share of experience at sea. "Amazing Grace" was a rear admiral in the United States Navy and a pioneer in computer science at a time when there were almost no women in the field. She believed that "The most damaging phrase in the language is: 'It's always been done that way.'" When you're trying to find the happiness on the other side of the hit you've taken, this phrase can be especially insidious. It can sneak its way into your thoughts or your decision-making process and undermine your resilience. Just because "It's always been done this way" doesn't mean that there aren't other or better ways to do something. In fact, being overly reliant on customs, traditions, and family and cultural patterns will prevent you from discovering your own authentic path. Take a few minutes to consider consistency's influence on your own life:

- Are you stuck in a relationship rut? Just because things have always been a certain way in the past doesn't mean that you can't begin doing things differently. Relationships can— and *should*—be renegotiated as the parties involved evolve. There are many different ways to be married, to be sexual, to be friends, and to be involved with people. Don't feel guilty about initiating change in your relationships—you're doing all parties involved a great service if you're moving things toward more authenticity. Don't let an insistence on consistency ruin your relationships.

- Are you professionally paralyzed? Most people spend more hours working every week than doing any other single thing (even sleeping!). Your time here on Planet Earth is really, really valuable, and you should spend it as wisely and authentically as possible. If you're not fulfilled in your career or if your work doesn't allow "the real you" any room to come out, sticking with it out of fear of change is a terribly "foolish consistency." Everyone has bad days and they call work *work* for a reason, but deep down, you know if you should be exploring other options. Just because you've always made a living one way doesn't mean there aren't other ways to get the job done. (The next chapter deals with this issue in-depth, so keep reading.)

- Have you been caught by the parent trap? If you have kids, it's very easy to get stuck in parenting patterns that someone else came up with but that don't really work for you. The two biggest snares to watch out for: letting your own upbringing or "family traditions" limit your choices as a parent by focusing too much on the way "it's always been done" and getting caught up in a kind of competitive parenting where you feel pressured to do things the way "everyone else" is doing them.

- Are you in a spiritual slump? Just because you were raised in a particular religious tradition doesn't mean that it's the only way for you to connect with your spirit. Just because you've been attending the same weekly service for the last fifteen years doesn't mean that you can't do things differently in the future.

- And just because all your friends or neighbors spend Sunday mornings doing one thing, it doesn't mean that you can't do your own thing. There is no virtue in sticking with the spiritual status quo if you're really just going through the motions. Clinging to consistency in this area can prevent you from ever finding an authentic spiritual path. You owe it to yourself to keep it real.

Do any of these questions resonate with you? Does the idea of doing things differently excite you? Even if you're ready to reconsider consistency, the idea of change can make you nervous. If you've taken a serious hit, it can be tempting to just stick with the status quo because it's what you know and because, frankly, you're tired. You also might be afraid of other people's reactions. This is totally normal, but now is the time to face your fear and find the authentic happiness on the other side of the hit you've taken.

Tribal Tribulations

We all like to think of ourselves as being "independently owned and operated." After all, as Dwight D. Eisenhower points out, "Here in America we are descended in spirit from revolutionists and rebels—men and women who dare to dissent from accepted doctrine." But do we really dare to dissent as much as we imagine? Very few people ever allow themselves to depart from the road most traveled. Most people make the mistaken assumption that they're on the right road just because it's a well-beaten path.

Even if you want to do things your own way, you'll undoubtedly experience pressure to stay consistent and to conform. Often, this pressure comes from the people closest to you. Voltaire hits the nail on the head when he writes that "Our wretched species is so made that those who walk on the well-trodden path always throw stones at those who are showing a new road." If you try to "show a new road" by breaking with tradition or questioning authority, you may get some stones thrown at you from people and directions that might surprise you. If you want to tap into your bulletproof spirit, you've got to be willing to keep walking no matter what flies your way. You'll have to learn to duck and dodge because there will always be critics when you dare to do things differently. If you can summon the courage to say no to the "road most traveled," you will be able to begin the most important leg of your journey—the one that takes you down the road to your authentic destiny. Many people toy with the idea of taking "the road less traveled," but very few are willing to actually pay the toll.

One of the most significant milestones in your spiritual journey is being willing to pay the price of losing the approval of other people. Dependence upon the approval of your family, friends, and society in general is a kind of prison that can stunt your spiritual evolution and prevent you from rebounding from adversity. As Friedrich Nietzsche puts it:

> *The individual has always had to struggle to keep from being overwhelmed by the tribe. If you try it, you will be lonely often, and sometimes frightened. But no price is too high to pay for the privilege of owning yourself.*

If you want to "own yourself," you must be willing to risk the disapproval of the tribe. Resisting the pressure of the tribe can take many different forms, from the most dramatic to the most mundane. While it can be truly terrifying to depart from the tribe, it gets easier the more you do it. If you start with small things and work your way up, you'll realize that, even though it can be lonely or scary, there's no other way to live an authentic life. You'll also realize that the *thought* of change or not conforming is often more frightening than the actual act of doing it.

Confessions of a Consistency Drop-Out

Much as we can convince ourselves otherwise, the truth is that no one really cares all that much what you do, so you may as well do what you want to do. When you've taken enough hits, you *will* eventually get to the point where you no longer care what anyone thinks of you and what you do. Even if you're not really there yet, why not act as if you are? Why not begin to live the way you want to live right now? How many hits are you willing to take before you realize that the time to live the life you imagine is right now? Are you really willing to sacrifice your authenticity just so that people will approve of you? Margaret Mitchell was right when she said "Until you've lost your reputation, you never realize what a burden it was."

Nothing bad happens when you stop clinging to consistency as though it were a virtue. And don't think that it's only the "big things" that make the difference in whether you live an authentic life; in fact, we've found that the cumulative effect of lots of small departures from the status quo and the tribe can add up to a life that's real. Pay attention to the little tyrannies that rein you in—give yourself permission to choose authentically when it comes to the "little things," and you'll see that they really do start to add up to a life that's your own. Here are a few examples of the kind of "little inconsistencies" I've engaged in that, while I agonized over them at the time, ended up creating no repercussions whatsoever despite all the warnings the tribe gave me to the contrary:

- I've quit jobs that "people would kill for" and turned down job offers that "people would die for" so that I could actually have time to do the work my soul could no longer live without. And guess what? I'm still standing, no one's dead, and I can pay my bills.
- I've taken my kids out of the public schools, homeschooled them, and then even sent them back again—major depar-

tures from the way "it's always been done" in my family and among our friends. And guess what? Everyone can still read, write, do arithmetic, and socialize normally. In the end, the whole thing was just a blip on everyone else's radar screen.

- I've resisted overscheduling my kids over the years and didn't sign them up for all the teams, clubs, lessons, and activities that "everyone else" was doing. And guess what? They are having a relaxed, old-fashioned childhood and are well-rounded, secure, and good at lots of things. They also have inner lives that had a chance to blossom because they weren't on the run all the time.

When I refuse to do something just because everyone else is doing it, I sometimes do encounter disapproval and criticism. Friends, neighbors, other parents, even my *own* parents question my choices. I just keep ducking and dodging the stones that come my way and I do my own thing. And I'm a thin-skinned, sensitive scaredy-cat—if I can kick consistency to the curb, so can you!

It isn't always easy going against the tide. It can definitely be a little lonely on the "road less traveled." But there are many different "right" ways to do things and some of the best things will happen when you reconsider consistency and commit yourself to authenticity. Fear of disapproval should not be the compass by which you navigate your life. And when you dare to depart from the tribe, you will not be alone. You'll be with all the other people who've dared to do things differently, and most of the tribe will come around in the end anyway. As American financier Bernard Baruch reminds us: "Those who matter don't mind and those who mind don't matter."

Your bulletproof spirit wants you to live the life you were meant to live. One way to give meaning to the heartbreaking hits you've taken is to use them to motivate you to rebuild an authentic life. While it can feel scary to do things differently or to risk not fitting in, making the choice to be true to yourself is actually the safest thing you can do. Living by someone else's rules or according to someone else's vision is not really living at all. Let the hits you've taken remind you that there's no time to waste. What are you waiting for?

• • •

Bounce Back Boot Camp

Here are some ideas to help you kick consistency to the curb:

- Use your journal to create a list of the people in your "tribe." Get clear about who is in this "circle of influence." Consider family, friends, neighbors, colleagues from work, people from church, people you grew up knowing, people from organizations you belong to. Consider how much you truly care about what each of these people or groups think. Whose approval really matters to you? Make a list in which you rank these people and groups according to how great an influence they have upon your decision making. Then look at the top three names on your list. Think about how much or how little the approval of these people matters to you. Ask yourself the following questions:

  - Are you afraid of losing their approval?
  - What is the worst thing that would happen if you did lose their approval?
  - Do any of these people have strong opinions about the "right" way to do things?
  - Do you think that you make choices based upon your fear of these people thinking less of you?
  - What, if anything, might you change if none of these people were in the picture?
  - What would you do or not do if you were free from their influence?

Pay careful attention to your responses to these questions—start to become more aware of the influence "the tribe" has over you. Remind yourself that you can act independently from the tribe if you choose to. Finish this exercise by telling yourself "The most important approval I seek is my own."

- Take your calendar out and look at the last three months. Tally up all the things on it that you did because you were afraid of departing from the tribe. Be really honest with yourself. Count up the number of days that you've sacrificed at the altar of other people's opinion. I'm not talking about obligations that you just didn't feel like taking care of, like getting your teeth cleaned or paying your taxes. I'm referring to the things you spent time doing because of habit, custom, tradition, or other people's expectations and not because they really fit in with your own vision of an authentic life. You may be amazed at how much of your life you regularly sign away because of your unwillingness to depart from the status quo. On the other hand, this exercise may just confirm what you already knew and are finally getting ready to act upon.

- Is there a "road less traveled" that you've been wanting to go down? Again, use your journal to explore a path that you might be afraid to take in real life. Is there some area of your life where you'd like to make a change but don't because of a "foolish consistency"? Ask yourself "If no one was 'watching' and I couldn't fail, what would I do differently?" Your answer to this question is very important—it can point you in the direction of a more authentic life. Don't worry, you don't need to actually do anything right now. Just let yourself begin to think about the fact that there is more than one "right way" to do anything: There are *lots* of right ways to work, love, parent, have fun, contribute, and live, and you owe it to yourself to find the ones that are authentically you.

• • •

Connect with Your Calling

Each person has their own calling on this Earth.

—BILLY RAY CYRUS

SPIRITUALLY FRAGILE PEOPLE COMPARTMENTALIZE THEIR WORK AND desire for personal fulfillment—their work means a paycheck and they try to find meaning in other areas of their lives. They don't connect the dots. This can leave them feeling fragmented, overwhelmed, and unable to really express their authentic selves. Spiritually bulletproof people search for and find ways to integrate these two elements. They believe that each person has a particular "calling" and they make it their business to hear and respond to their own. Bouncing back means more than just recovering from grief and pain—it means re-creating yourself and your life. Finding your own "calling" and responding to it will help steer you toward the happiness that's on the other side of the hit you've taken.

You may think that a "calling" is something reserved for people who want to pursue religious vocations or other "lofty" ambitions; you may not hear any "calling" calling to *you*. But connecting with your own calling is actually a down-to-earth, practical endeavor—it's about integrating the competing pieces of your life. It's about finding a way to do what makes you happy, make a living, and make the world a better place all at once. As much as possible, spiritually bulletproof people integrate work and personal fulfillment by finding and following their calling.

> Spiritually bulletproof people integrate work and personal fulfillment by finding and following their calling.

When you're trying to rebound from your crisis or loss, connecting with your calling can help you create the momentum you need to begin again. Rebuilding your life after a major hit is a little like rebuilding a house after it burns to the ground. If your house burned down and you got insurance money to rebuild, wouldn't you take advantage of the opportunity to start over by making sure that your new house really suited you? Since you'd be taking the trouble to start all over again, wouldn't it be worth the effort it takes to plan a house that functions perfectly for your lifestyle and your needs? Well, one upside of hits is that they essentially force you to start over. Now is the time to rebuild your life so that it better suits you and your needs. Now is the time to find and follow your calling and integrate the different pieces of your life.

Mission Possible

If you feel a little daunted by the prospect of trying to find your "calling," the word "mission" might be more user-friendly to you. Think of a mission as a special assignment given to a person—one that the person is especially suited to perform and that affects the larger world. When you think of missions, you probably think of *Mission: Impossible*—"Your mission, should you choose to accept it . . ."—and its invitation to intrigue, adventure, and danger. But not all missions are so serious. In the film *The Blues Brothers,* Dan Aykroyd's character, Elwood, and John Belushi's character, Jake, are being pursued by the police when Elwood reassures Jake by telling him "They're not gonna catch us. We're on a mission from God." The line gets a huge laugh from the audience, but Elwood is dead serious. There are as many "missions" as there are people on the planet, and there is one out there with your name on it . . . if you dare to accept it.

Getting in touch with your own personal mission by creating a mission statement can be one of the most powerful ways of beginning again after a serious hit. A mission statement is simply a short written articulation of your goals and values. Mission statements were popularized by Dr. Stephen Covey in his book *The Seven Habits of Highly Effective People.* Here's what Dr. Covey says about the benefit of developing your own mission statement:

> *It's like deciding first which wall you want to lean your ladder of life against, and then beginning to climb. It will be a compass—a strong source of guidance amid the stormy seas and pressing, pulling currents of your life.*

As you begin to get more conscious about your goals and values, your own calling, purpose, or mission in life will start to come into focus. The key is to figure out where your goals and your values *intersect.* (Read that sentence again and let it percolate.) It's not enough to know what you *want*—you need to be clear about what really *matters* to you and who you really *are.*

Catholic missionary Sister Ita Ford said "I hope you come to find that which gives life a deep meaning for you. Something worth living for—maybe even worth dying for. Something that energizes you, enthuses you, and enables you to keep moving ahead. I can't tell you what it might be—that's for you to find, to choose, to love. I can just encourage you to start looking, and support you in the search." Spiritually bulletproof people make it a priority to find that "something worth living for" and this *does* enable'them to keep moving ahead no matter what obstacles they face or what hits come their way. No one can tell you what that "something" is, but finding it for yourself is one of the critical milestones in your spiritual journey.

The calling that's calling you is uniquely suited to your particular goals and values. It is perfectly designed to accommodate your greatest joy while simultaneously meeting a genuine need out in the world. American minimalist composer La Monte Young expresses a view common to people who have found and are following their calling when he says "I had a calling to become what I became—I was created to do this." What were you "created to do"? Your calling doesn't have to be toward something dramatic, larger-than-life, or impressive to other people. As Oliver Wendell Holmes points out "Every calling is great when greatly pursued."

Love Made Visible

Spiritually resilient people find and follow their callings no matter where they lead. A calling doesn't always lead to a "job," in the traditional sense of that word. Catholic priest and theologian Matthew Fox says that "A job is something we do to get a paycheck and pay our bills. Jobs are legitimate, at times, but work is why we are here in the universe. Work and calling often go together." It's important to note that "work" doesn't always mean "paycheck." For example, though I feel called to a few different things as part of my life's purpose, one of the strongest callings I feel is to be a parent. Twelve years into this "job," I have yet to receive a single paycheck, although the rewards I receive are great, indeed. As you try to connect with your own calling, don't limit yourself with the idea that your calling must translate directly into paid work. The poet Kahlil Gibran expands the definition of work when he writes "Work is love made visible."

How do you make your love and your light visible in the world? Do you teach children? Do you care for sick people? Do you fix cars? Do you make money to give people what they need? Do you recycle? Do you design things? Do you keep things running? Do you speak kindly? There are as many ways to "work" as there are people on the planet. The things you love to do are clues about your calling. You can bet that there is a need out there in the world that you can fill by making your love "visible."

While not all *authentic* work translates itself into *paid* work, it is lovely and convenient when the two collide. Doing something for the love of it and getting paid for the doing of it is one of the nicest, most miraculous intersections imaginable. I think of well-known people like Oprah, J. K. Rowling, and Joel Osteen, who seem to have found this intersection, but I also think of Tim, the manager of a quick mart I frequent, and my longtime babysitter, Katie, as well as my husband, who teaches seventh-grade social studies—regular people who have found the extraordinary joy of making a living doing what they love. Authentic work is an equal-opportunity employer. It truly is possible for you to make a living by following your calling, but you must *believe* that it's possible.

It's very easy to end up spending your life doing work that does nothing more than pay you money. And while there *are* times when it's necessary to do whatever you have to do to make ends meet, you can and should aim to integrate making a living with following your calling. As writer Rita Mae Brown cautions "Don't trade the stuff of your life—time—for nothing more than dollars. That's a rotten bargain." Theologian Frederick Buechner defines a calling as the intersection where "your great gladness meets the world's great need." Spiritually bulletproof people go looking for that intersection and they also believe there will be an ATM on the corner. Mark Twain gets to the heart of this idea when he writes "What work I have done I have done because it has been play . . . The work that is really a man's own work is play and not work at all . . . When we talk about the great work-

ers of the world we really mean the great players of the world."
What do you love to "play" at that happens to fill a real need out
in the world? If you spend some time trying to find that intersection, you will be amazed at where the road leads.

Ultimately, connecting with your calling is one of the best
ways to feed your bulletproof spirit. Career guru and author
Marsha Sinetar believes that "Burning desire to be or do something gives us staying power—a reason to get up every morning
or to pick ourselves up and start in again after a disappointment."
That burning desire to do or be something is what a calling is all
about. Find yours and watch how high you'll bounce.

• • •

Bounce Back Boot Camp

Here are some simple suggestions to help you connect with your
calling:

- Getting clear about your "mission" can motivate you and
  point you in the right direction as you begin to rise from
  the ashes and rebuild your life. If you've never written a
  mission statement, now is the perfect time for you to do so.
  You can make it very simple. Start by answering three simple questions:

  - What are my personal and professional goals?
  - What will I do to meet those goals?
  - What values or beliefs guide my choices?

    Start by responding in your journal to these three
  questions. Write as much as you like and try to get all of
  your ideas down on paper. Next, create a clear, concise
  summary of your most important points. Try to get each
  of your three responses down to no more than two sen-
  tences. Now, massage the language and "flow" of your answers so that you create one coherent message. Read it a

number of times and see if it reflects your goals and values. The statement should inspire you when you read it over, so consider it a work-in-progress until you are happy with it. Azim wrote a mission statement before his son died but found that he needed to rewrite it after his life-altering tragedy. Both times, he referred to the work of Dr. Stephen Covey. For more ideas to get you started on your mission statement, we highly recommend that you visit Dr. Covey's website at www.stephencovey.com and check out his life-changing books and online resources.

- Use your journal and brainstorm about the following fill-in-the-blank statements:

  If I did what I loved, I would _____.
  If I knew I couldn't fail, I would _____.
  What makes me really joyful is _____.
  Something that I think the world really needs is _____.
  If my love were made visible, it would look like _____.

  Don't overthink your responses—just see what comes up for you. Give yourself permission to fantasize and think outside the box.

- If you're ready to connect with your own calling, author and teacher Marsha Sinetar is an invaluable resource. Her books *Do What You Love, The Money Will Follow* and *Holy Work* will coach you through the process of finding your calling. Check her out at www.MarshaSinetar.com.

- Many people find their calling on the path of service. Ask yourself how your unique package of skills, experiences, and passions can assist other people. You may find that the hits you've taken have prepared you to offer service to others in similar circumstances. Begin to reach out to others and see what unfolds—many, many people find their true calling by helping other people come out on top of their own hits.

• • •

Part Five

. . .

BULLETPROOF BEST PRACTICES

Say Yes to Your Adventure

*The big question is whether you are going to
be able to say a hearty yes to your adventure.*

—Joseph Campbell

IF YOU WANT TO BE SPIRITUALLY BULLETPROOF, YOU NEED TO BE-
lieve that you and your life actually *matter* in the grand scheme of
things. If you don't believe this, you are going to have a hard
time dealing with adversity because all the heartbreaking hits life
hands you will feel like meaningless suffering.

Viktor Frankl, a psychiatrist who lost almost all his family in
the concentration camps in Nazi Germany, believed that "Those
who have a 'why' to live can bear with almost any 'how.'" Spiritually resilient people have a strong sense of "why" they're living. Spiritually bulletproof people think of themselves as heroes
on a kind of quest. All that happens to them, good and bad, is
part of the myth they see themselves living.

This doesn't mean that they have delusions of grandeur or
that they think of themselves as being any better or more special

> Spiritually bulletproof people think of themselves as heroes on a kind of quest. All that happens to them, good and bad, is part of the myth they see themselves living.

than anyone else. In fact, they are famous for annoying their less-optimistic friends by seeing *them* as heroes on a grand adventure, too!

World-renowned mythologist Joseph Campbell believed that "Myths are public dreams, dreams are private myths," and spiritually resilient people see their lives as privately unfolding myths intertwined with the privately unfolding myths of everyone else around them. They consciously create mythic constructs for their lives by reframing heartbreaking hits as twists or turns in the plots of their spiritual sagas.

Saying Yes to Your Adventure

It can feel really weird at first to think of yourself as a hero on a quest and it can seem downright crazy to say *yes* to an experience or situation thrust upon you by a heartbreaking hit. But if you want the benefits that come with spiritual resiliency, you're going to need to look at things in a whole new way. Spiritually bulletproof people are able to see that invitations to adventure often come disguised as heartbreaking hits. These invitations arrive unbidden and unwelcome, but spiritually resilient people open them up and will themselves to say *yes* even though they may be freaking out inside at first.

If you stop and think about it, most of the heroes we love in literature, movies, or real life begin their true adventures or set out on their quests after receiving an invitation in the form of a hit. In the movie *Braveheart,* Mel Gibson's character, William Wallace, is invited to the quest of a lifetime by the death of his beloved wife. He sees in this terrible loss that he is called to an adventure he wouldn't have chosen, but that is his destiny. Actor

Michael J. Fox didn't view his diagnosis with Parkinson's disease as the *end* of his life—he recognized that he was being called to an altogether different adventure than the one he had planned. Though it wasn't immediate or easy, he said *yes* to a quest that has already impacted the world in a more profound way than he would have been able to without his diagnosis.

You might be thinking to yourself, "Well, I'm not a movie star or a warrior, so I can't really relate. I'm just ordinary—not heroic." But when spiritually bulletproof people watch Mel Gibson as William Wallace in *Braveheart* or Will Smith as Chris Gardner in *The Pursuit of Happyness,* they *identify* with what they see playing on the big screen. They are not deluded or in some kind of fantasy world—they are just very connected to their inner heroes. Movies like these are blockbusters because the heroes in them speak to *all* of us in some very primal way. But for spiritually resilient people, the connection is more conscious. They know that there really is only one story being told in every great book written, movie made, or life lived: the story of a hero who says *yes* to the adventure, endures all sorts of trials, and goes on to achieve something or to *become* someone. We keep creating and responding to art that tells this story because, deep down, we know that it is *our* story, too.

Because our real-life stories may be less dramatic than the ones in the movies, we may not realize that the same mythic construct is at work. I coached a man named Paul who worked with a man who sexually harassed the women in his department to such a degree that he felt obligated to get involved and report him. It turned out that the harasser belonged to an extremely strong union that protected him from being fired. Paul had to continue to work with this toxic person, who now made daily violent threats against him. He tried all the avenues available to him to get the guy disciplined or removed, but in the end, nothing worked and he was stuck working with this scary character. Paul didn't want to resign because he would lose his benefits, the salary he needed to support his family, and even his pension because he wasn't yet vested, but ultimately he did quit so that he could regain his mental health and quality of life. This was a serious hit for Paul—he lost his professional identity, his financial security, and also experienced tension in his marriage because his wife worried about what they would do without his salary. This all happened at a time when jobs in his field were scarce and the economy was tight. He felt paralyzed with rage at both the harasser and his former employer and also anxious because he had no idea what to do next, which was causing tremendous friction in his marriage.

We worked together on a number of issues. We did the kind of grieving work covered in Secret 8 and we also used the ideas and strategies covered in Secrets 14 through 17 to help Paul release his anger and pain through the power of forgiveness and self-forgiveness. But one of the most beneficial and dramatic changes he made was reframing what had happened to him and finding the invitation to adventure that was hiding below the surface of the hit he had taken. With coaching, Paul began to see that he could come out on top if he said *yes* to a new adventure that he had not sought but that had his name written all over it.

One of the things that bothered him most about the whole situation at his former job was witnessing many of his female colleagues struggle with the unwelcome advances of the harasser. He had actually gotten involved in the first place because very few women affected knew what to do when faced with such an aggressive bully. Paul also had black belts in a number of the martial arts, but over the years, it had become harder and harder to find time for his passion. We began to explore the possibilities that the hit he took had opened up, and six months later, Paul started a business whose mission is to empower women by giving them the tools and practice they need to keep themselves safe and to create healthy boundaries. He uses his expertise in martial arts and his background in education to create his programs, but the fuel that fires the whole thing is the workplace crisis that forced such change. He has a thriving consulting business and he has even appeared as a personal safety and assertiveness expert on television shows. He loves his new career, and is no longer angry or anxious, and his marriage has grown tremendously because of his journey. It all started with his willingness to say *yes* to the adventure that was hiding inside the hit he had taken.

The Road of Trials

When spiritually bulletproof people say *yes* to the adventure put in front of them, it doesn't mean that everything suddenly gets easy and goes smoothly. To the contrary, saying *yes* can actually seem to make things harder at first. When a hit calls them to an adventure and they say *yes,* they step upon what Joseph Campbell calls "the road of trials." They may not use these actual words or know anything about mythology at all, but they *do* know that the road in front of them will present them with obstacles and problems and suffering. Spiritually resilient people *know* that any adventure they take on will bring with it difficulties, so they handle them better when they come along.

When I lost my third baby late in pregnancy, I said *yes* to the invitation I found hidden in that heartbreak and found myself on the road to international adoption. *Believe* me when I say that it brought me more trials than the Enron scandal! The red tape, fingerprinting, homeland security clearances, lost documents, immunizations, delays, avian flu warnings, and translation snafus were just the tip of the iceberg. I also met with emotional hurdles every single step of the way on my journey to my daughter on the other side of the world. But when I said *yes* to the adventure, I was committing to the problems that came with it. If you want to raise your spiritual-resiliency quotient, begin to look at the struggles or trials you face as an integral part of your adventure.

Spiritually resilient people also know that there is a reliable pattern at work in the universe: When they face an obstacle and surmount it, they are rewarded with new knowledge, personal power, or wisdom. Awareness of this pattern allows them to reframe the hits they take as not only a natural part of life, but even as vehicles for spiritual growth.

Think about all the lessons you've learned in your life up to now. If you're like most people, you learned many of those important lessons the hard way—through problems and suffering that you had to endure and get past. You've been living the life of a hero on a grand adventure all along, but you didn't consciously acknowledge it. It's much easier to see the quest your life has been—the adventure you said *yes* to—in retrospect. Looking back, you can probably identify many hits you took that, in the end, taught you what you needed to know or took you where you needed to go next. It's actually pretty simple to see the meaning in your past. The trick is to see the same meaning in your present.

• • •

Bounce Back Boot Camp

Here are three exercises for you to do to connect with your inner hero:

- Work this first exercise in with your leisure time and have fun with it. Rent *Braveheart, Gandhi, The Count of Monte Cristo, The Lord of the Rings, The Pursuit of Happyness,* or *Forrest Gump.* Or better yet, rent *all* of them! If you have any other favorite hero movies, include them, too. (If you experiment, you'll actually find that almost every movie is a kind of hero story.) Make it fun for yourself—make a big bowl of popcorn and get comfy. As you watch the films, look for the patterns this chapter points out. After each movie, write in your journal about the hero's heartbreaking hit(s). Do you relate to any of the heroes or the hits they take? Did they learn any lessons you connect with?

Find one idea or quality to borrow from each hero and write about it.

- Use your computer or your artistic skills to create a special invitation. The invitation is *from* your heartbreaking hit and it is addressed *to* you. Where is it asking you to go or what is it asking you to do? Let your mind be free as you make the invitation and be as creative as you can. Remember, it's the *process* you engage in while doing these activities that is healing and empowering, so don't get hung up on the finished product.
- Make a list with two columns. On the left side, list all the heartaches, heartbreaks, failures, losses, and other "bullets" you've taken. On the right side, list the corresponding lessons, wisdom, insights, knowledge, and personal growth that came from living through and surmounting those hits. Be as exhaustive as you can. Include stuff from the seventh grade. Write the phrase TRIALS AND REVELATIONS in bold print at the top. Hang the list where you'll see it and reread it at least once a day. Add to the list if you want to.

Note: If you visit our website you can download a list of great hero movies to help you connect with your inner hero. There are also links to a number of sites to visit if you're interested in learning more about the mythic pattern of the hero's journey. We've also included links to some great "Cinematherapy" information and books for you to check out.

• • •

Pay Attention to Your Attractions

I will not hide my tastes or aversions.
I will so trust that what is deep is holy,
that I will do strongly before the sun and moon
whatever inly rejoices me, and the heart appoints.

—RALPH WALDO EMERSON

SPIRITUALLY BULLETPROOF PEOPLE CONSCIOUSLY NOTE AND GIVE
energy to their attractions to people, things, and situations. On
the flip side of this equation, they also notice and act upon their
aversions. The word *attraction* may bring to mind the idea of romantic or sexual attraction, but for our purposes here, think of
attraction in a broader and deeper way. Attraction is an intuitive
sense that draws you toward not only people, but experiences,
situations, and things as well. Attraction refers to anything that
interests you, resonates within you, or that you feel drawn
toward, often for reasons you don't quite understand. For example, I've always been attracted to Asian cultures and philosophies,
but could never articulate why. But I consciously note and honor
my attractions and, though it took twenty years, I eventually

came to understand how this attraction was connected, as all attractions are, to my destiny. People with low spiritual resiliency tend to be out of touch with, resistant to, or outright rejecting of their own preferences and dislikes. Changing your thinking in this area can turbo-charge your ability to bounce back from heartbreak or loss, and can also fuel the fulfillment of your dreams.

> Spiritually bulletproof people pay attention to their attractions and aversions and honor them in thought and deed.

"When you follow your bliss," writes Joseph Campbell, "doors will open where you would not have thought there would be doors, and where there wouldn't be a door for anyone else." If you want to find and open the door to the new life on the other side of whatever hit you've taken, make up your mind to take up a new thinking habit, one that resilient people either innately or consciously practice: Spiritually bulletproof people pay attention to their attractions and aversions and honor them in thought and deed.

If you want to be physically healthy, you need to pay attention to your body's signals. For example, if you are tired, it's a wiser choice to rest than to fuel up with caffeine. And if you have pain in your knee when you run, it's smarter to have it checked out than to keep running. The cumulative effect of listening to your body's signals over the years is health and vitality, while the cumulative effect of ignoring your body's signals is injury, disease, or burnout. In much the same way, our spiritual resiliency and personal fulfillment are impacted by how well and how consistently we pay attention to our spirit's signals.

An Attraction Is a Spiritual Signal

Spiritually fragile people are not fluent in the language of spirit. Your ability to surmount crisis is strongly connected to how well you can communicate with your spirit, which is an unlimited well of resiliency. Your spirit utilizes many forms of communication, but one way it tries to speak to you is through your attractions and aversions.

Most people walk around unable or unwilling to receive their souls' signals. Their souls are like radio stations sending out important messages over the airwaves, but their minds are like radios that aren't plugged in. People want to know how to respond to relationships, how to handle the situations they face, and what they should do with their lives, but they don't realize that the answers to these pressing questions are being sent to them in secret code in the form of their own attractions and aversions. In theory, all of this seems like a very basic form of self-awareness, but in real life, lots of things get in the way. Here are a few reasons why you might not be acting on your attractions:

- Maybe your parents or other people told you that the things you liked or wanted were out of your league or unattainable. If you believe that your desires are unachievable, they go undercover. Many people have a hard time even *talking* about what they're attracted to because they won't allow themselves to "get their hopes up." We've had many, many students and clients over the years who were closet artists, writers, and performers but who never openly pursued those desires because they believed parents, teachers, or other dream-crushers who told them that their attractions were unrealistic. (By the way, many of them went on to actually fulfill their dreams and impact the world in fabulous ways once they allowed themselves to follow their bliss.)

- You might judge certain attractions to be unacceptable and, therefore, not allow yourself to follow them. One woman I coached was very attracted to money, but had grown up believing that people who liked money were bad. She worked in low-paying service jobs that didn't fulfill her and felt guilty because she was secretly fascinated by the stock market. When she was finally able to honor her own attractions, she took a job in finance and her career took off. It turns out that she was *made* to make money, much of which she actually gives away to worthy causes! It took her twenty years to allow herself to *be* herself because she had been programmed to think that her attractions were unacceptable. This is *very* common and *very* sad! (Note: This section refers to *healthy* attractions, not behaviors that are hurtful in any way to yourself or others.)

- Sometimes it's our *aversions* that we're not paying attention to. Many people spend their time and energy doing things they do not like and may even hate. One woman I worked with spent more than a decade in a relationship with a man who she disliked having sex with. She didn't realize that her body was trying to tell her something important about what direction she should take in terms of relationships. If you really can't stand something, you must pay attention to it! It's trying to tell you something.

Getting back in touch with your attractions and aversions can put you on the fast track to greater spiritual resiliency. In fact, spiritually bulletproof people use their own attractions and aversions as a kind of navigation system—they reliably steer them *toward* experiences they're meant to have and *away* from people, things, and situations that would only distract them from their destiny. This navigation system is constantly coaching you toward your highest good, but it does you no good if you don't notice or listen to what it's telling you. Sometimes you just need to get out of your own way!

While spiritually fragile people may not even know what attracts them or they may ignore those attractions, spiritually bulletproof people are intimately acquainted with their deepest desires and they trust them *completely*. They don't waste energy questioning or doubting their attractions, and they certainly don't worry if what attracts them is very different from what attracts other people. Resilient people don't care what other people think about their attractions and they don't allow themselves to be intimidated out of them. They rightly know that their own healthy attractions and aversions come from a holy place inside themselves, and this keeps them going in the right direction.

Attractions Are Doors

Being able to take a hit and come out on top requires being able to make inspired choices at critical moments. How do you know whether a choice is an inspired one? First, it must make sense to your head. Second, it must feel right in your heart. And third, it must be exciting to your spirit. People often neglect this third part of the equation. Attraction is all about what's exciting to your spirit, so following your attractions helps you make inspired choices. If something makes sense "on paper," but you're not attracted to it, it is almost never the right decision.

Acting on attractions can also require a leap of faith. Sometimes it is not clear where an attraction will lead, so you need to be willing to remain unattached to outcome. Sometimes our attractions do not even make *sense* to us—we just experience a strange and unexplainable pull toward something or someone and feel compelled to act on it. When this happens to spiritually fragile people, they often let their heads overrule their attractions because they mistakenly believe that their brains can outsmart their own spirits. But when spiritually bulletproof people experience an attraction that they can't immediately understand or make sense of, they know better than to ignore it or override it with their intellects. They leap out in faith, trusting that more will be revealed in the fullness of time. (One caveat: Again, we're talking here about attractions that are healthy for all parties involved.)

Here's what paying attention to your attractions and aversions might look like:

- You might make a point to strike up a conversation with a person you find attractive, knowing that there are many reasons why people are drawn together and being open to the possibilities . . .

- You might sign up for a class or course in a subject you've always been interested in knowing more about, knowing that more may be revealed if you just take a first step toward your attraction . . .

- You might plan a day trip to a neighborhood you feel drawn to or a vacation to a country that's always fascinated you, knowing that sometimes you have to be in the right place at the right time . . .

- You might stop going to a doctor whom all your friends and family like just because he's always made you inexplicably uncomfortable, knowing that your intuitive dislikes serve to protect you in ways you cannot always understand . . .

Following your attractions and honoring your aversions will get easier and more natural for you the more you do it. Start with small things, and when you see how well your attractions serve you, you'll get more confident. When crisis strikes, there are often moments that are *defining* moments, or opportunities to make an inspired choice that leads to healing for yourself and possibly for others. Paying attention to your attractions can help you make an inspired choice in a defining moment, and that can make all the difference in whether you come out on top of a hit. Paying attention to my own affinity for Asian culture did, in the end, help me make an inspired choice at a defining moment. My inner navigation system led me to the daughter I was destined to mother—she just happened to be on the other side of the world in China.

• • •

Bounce Back Boot Camp

Try these techniques for tapping into the power of your attractions:

- Get in touch with what attracts you. Make a collage or montage of people, things, symbols, ideas, and images that attract you. Gather a bunch of magazines that interest you and spend an evening browsing through them and clipping out anything that catches your eye or attracts you. Do not overanalyze your choices or censor yourself in any way. Arrange and glue the clippings on a piece of sturdy oak tag or cardboard, letting yourself group or place the images in any way that feels right or interesting to you. When you're done, put your masterpiece somewhere you can reflect on it frequently. One woman I worked with hung hers on the inside of her master bathroom door!

- For one whole day—make it a weekend day if it'll be easier—allow yourself to honor your attractions and aversions *completely.* You may be surprised at how hard this may actually be for you to let yourself do. Discover how in or out of touch you are with your likes and dislikes. See where they lead you. This exercise is all about little things—what you wear, what you eat, what television shows you watch, who you want to connect with, what you want to avoid. Be vigilant—don't make any choices based on *should* or *shouldn't.*

- Confess to your journal any secret attractions or aversions. What would you be or do if you couldn't fail? Are there dreams you've buried because you think they're unrealistic or because other people don't approve? Do you privately detest any aspect of your life? Even if you are not yet ready to act on your attractions or aversions, give yourself uncensored freedom to confess to them in the safety of your own notebook. Let your truth bubble to the surface and start making friends with it.

•   •   •

Create a Resilience-Rich Environment

The greatest discovery of my generation is that man can
alter his life simply by altering his attitude of mind.

—WILLIAM JAMES

IF YOU WANT TO CONNECT WITH YOUR OWN BULLETPROOF SPIRIT, begin to surround yourself with messages that maximize your own resilience. Spiritually bulletproof people make sure that they feed themselves a steady diet of aspirational and inspirational words and images that help them develop, maintain, and expand their resilience. They consciously create "resilience-rich environments" for themselves that support them as they face life's inevitable hits. Spiritually fragile people undermine their own resilience by letting themselves be inundated with negative and defeating messages and by starving themselves of the kind of nurturing their minds and spirits need in order to best respond to life's stresses and crises.

Inspirational speaker Les Brown believes that "People don't live life 'as it is'—they live it 'as they are.' " Because they know that their internal reality is the lens through which they see the external world, spiritually bulletproof people consciously surround themselves with words and images that support spiritual resiliency.

Just like children or plants thrive in certain conditions, so does spiritual resilience. If you want to come out on top of the hits life hands you, there are simple things you can do to create an environment where your bulletproof spirit can flourish.

> Spiritually bulletproof people consciously surround themselves with words and images that support spiritual resiliency.

See Dick Run

If you are reading these words right now, you must have learned to read at some point. You probably don't remember exactly how the whole process unfolded, but you may have some vague memories of phonics workbooks or Dick-and-Jane-type primers. Doesn't it seem miraculous that children learn to read at all? Somewhere between four and seven, almost every child figures out the incredibly complex code that unlocks a whole world of knowledge and pleasure. Most of us learned to read using phonics-based systems, but for the last twenty years or so, there has been an increasing emphasis on what is called "whole-language" instruction. The basic idea is that if you immerse students in a "print-rich" environment, they will learn to read spontaneously. While there are critics of this approach, there is no doubt that surrounding kids with letters, words, signs, books, and all kinds of written stimuli helps them make the critical leap to literacy. It just makes sense.

We create environments all the time, whether we are conscious of it or not. Anyone who has ever tried to eat more healthfully or lose weight knows that stocking up on healthy food ups the odds of sticking to the plan. When you keep healthy food on hand, it's more likely that you'll make good choices. Obviously, the reverse is true as well. If you're trying to drop ten pounds before swimsuit season, filling the fridge with fried chicken and packing the pantry with party food seriously undermines your chances of succeeding. If you want to eat right, doesn't it make sense to take the time and make the effort to create a healthy eating environment for yourself?

Your environment has the power to shape your state of mind. Think about your bedroom. Imagine satin sheets on your bed, rose petals on the floor, candles around the room, and Barry White playing in the background. Now, rip the satin sheets off, vacuum up the rose petals, and blow out all the candles. Shut Barry off. Take stacks of bills, canceled checks, and memos from work and put them all over the bed. Put your computer and fax machine on a desk opposite your bed and bring in the halogen floor lamp so you can read all the fine print. Turn on *The News-Hour with Jim Lehrer.* Same room, two entirely different environments. You don't have to be an interior designer to figure out which one will nurture your romantic relationship.

If you want to maintain and expand the connection you're starting to have with your bulletproof spirit, start today to create your own resilience-rich environment.

Talking to Yourself

Boost your bulletproof spirit by watching your words. It is easy to forget the power of words and fall into verbal and reading habits that undermine our own resilience. Be conscious about the words you listen to, look at, and use—they really do affect you on every level. Here are some strategies for "talking to yourself" in a way that supports your resilience:

- Read inspirational books. You absolutely *must* keep self-help and inspirational books in your line of sight and in your reading routine on a *daily* basis. I know that keeping up with the *Wall Street Journal,* trade magazines, and your book club pick can clutter up your nightstand and your reading schedule, but make no mistake about it, spiritually bulletproof people make time and space for inspirational books. It really doesn't matter exactly which ones you read at any given time, just make sure that you are getting your daily dose. Books are not just paper and ink—they carry the love, wisdom, and energy of other bulletproof spirits and they will transmit this love, wisdom, and energy to you if you let them. Surround yourself with the words of wise, resilient people, and you will notice that you will be supported by their messages and their energy. Make sure that you keep inspirational books in your car and carry one in your purse or briefcase. Pass books on to friends and ask them to pass theirs on to you. Think of these books as your personal "board of advisors," always available to guide, motivate, challenge, or console you.

• Keep fear-inspiring or negative books or magazines out of your environment. It is possible to stay informed without reading what the doomsayers and gloom-spreaders have to say on the subject. Don't feed your mind junk.

• Pay attention to the words you *hear.* Get audio CDs of inspirational books and listen to them in the car. Don't listen to a lot of hyper, cynical talk radio. Find a few radio stations or programs that have positive, uplifting hosts and guests and tune in to them when you drive. Use your commuting time to feed your spirit, not to flood it with stressful messages.

• Think about the effect of the words you hear from other people and protect yourself from chronically negative talkers. Start eliminating contact with people whose words undermine your resilience—don't hang out with the gossipers or complainers at work and screen your phone calls at home so that you can pick and choose which conversations to have.

- Use words as visual reminders and cues. Put signs, song lyrics, poems, quotations, and other messages to yourself throughout your environment. Get a magnetic poetry kit and use words to inspire you every time you open your refrigerator. You can make these resilience reminders an attractive part of your surroundings—be creative. Remember, your home is *your* space—use it to support your resilience, not just to house your stuff or impress your friends.
- Watch the words that come out of your own mouth. Use the techniques we suggest in many of the previous chapters to break verbal habits that undermine your resilience. Get in the habit of verbalizing affirmations and intentions. Saying positive things *out loud* sends a powerful signal to your unconscious mind.

Your mind is always hungry for stimulation—feed it words that nourish your bulletproof spirit. On every level, you are what you eat.

Become Your Own Image Consultant

Humans have evolved so that our vision is our most developed sense. Visual imagery has a profound influence on the way we think, feel, and respond. Think about the way that Madison Avenue and pornography use visual imagery to influence human behavior by creating desire. Spiritually bulletproof people consciously create visual environments that support their spiritual well-being and evolution. They use the power of visualization to turbo-charge their own resilience. The power of visualization is undeniable—professional athletes use visualization techniques to boost their performance and scientists know that visualization techniques are so powerful that they allow people to affect their own heart rate and blood pressure. Embrace the fact that you are a visually oriented being. Whether you know it or not, you are always creating and responding to images. Why not consciously harness the power of visualization to help you find the happiness on the other side of the hit you've taken?

How and why does visualization work? Think about the way your own body functions. When you get a small cut on your finger, your body knows to send platelets and white blood cells to the injury. How does it "know" to do this? Well, your body uses a lot of biochemical "messengers" to get what it needs from any part of the body. A simple way of explaining this complex biochemical dance is to think of the body as having a kind of "intelligence" that, when it is working properly, allows it to repair and maintain itself so effortlessly and precisely that it seems like magic. One day you have a cut, the next you have a scab, and the day after, you're all better! Well, visualization techniques work because the universe has a kind of intelligence that is similar to the body's but on an infinitely grander scale. When you focus on or visualize something, you send "thought messengers" out into the "cosmic body"—the universe. Then, over time, your thoughts manifest themselves in material form. The universe is the "body" in which you exist—it is "listening" to everything you think and everything you say, and it sends what's needed, where it's needed, when it's needed. Think about the great inventions and scientific breakthroughs that have shaped our world—every one of them started with an idea or image in someone's mind. Not sure that you believe that what you focus on affects your material reality? Think about what Einstein had to say about how messages travel:

> *You see, wire telegraph is a kind of very, very long cat. You pull his tail in New York and his head is meowing in Los Angeles. Do you understand this? And radio operates exactly the same way: you send signals here, they receive them there. The only difference is that there is no cat.*

Think about the electronic impulses your cell phone and wireless Internet use to do their "magic." Do you realize that your thoughts are also electronic impulses that can be measured using modern technology? Is it so very hard to accept that your thoughts travel on waves in much the same way that other impulses do? The "magic" is actually quantum physics in action; modern science really does reveal a universe where thought brings matter into form. Once you understand the fact that the words and images in your mind are constantly sending messages to the universe around you, you'll want to make those messages as helpful to yourself as possible. Images are even more powerful messages than words—a picture really is worth a thousand words. Try some of these suggestions for using the power of visualization to boost your ability to bounce back from adversity and conquer your crisis:

- Some people have an easier time "seeing" images in their mind than do others. At first, simply use actual images to support your resilience. Look through magazines and clip out images that represent what you hope to attain. For example, if you want to bounce back from an illness and get strong and healthy again, find a picture that suggests robust health and put it somewhere you'll see it throughout your day. If you want to rebound from a financial hit, put up an image that suggests financial abundance and look at it whenever you can. Feeding your mind with these images is a powerful way to nourish your bulletproof spirit.

- Get more conscious about what you watch on television and about which movies you see. Ideally, you only feed your mind and spirit visual data that is uplifting, thought-provoking, and inspiring, or that makes you feel high-frequency feelings like love or compassion. Television and movies are incredibly powerful "programs" that feed your mind intense streams of visual data—be mindful about what you "upload." Anything that makes you laugh really hard is good.

- Find a photograph that reminds you of a time in your life when you were really happy and well. Frame that photo and put it where you'll see it frequently. Every time you look at it, remind yourself that you *are* that happiness and wellness. Visualize yourself feeling and expressing that joy and health more and more. Use the image to help you connect with the feeling-state.
- Try out a guided meditation to help you visualize yourself undergoing spiritual transformation. There are many excellent guided meditations available as CDs or podcasts, or online. Visit our website for some great resources and links.

Strengthen your bulletproof spirit by nourishing it with inspirational words and images. Feed your soul only healthful and positive messages. Remember, you create a resilience-rich environment minute by minute and choice by choice—empower yourself to choose only the best.

• • •

Bounce Back Boot Camp

Start creating your own resilience-rich environment today by trying these ideas:

- Raise your image-consciousness. Look around your environment for opportunities to feed your spirit images that support your resilience. Look at simple things like your screen saver, your framed photos, and your artwork. Can you integrate any images that help you visualize the happiness that's on the other side of your hit? Introduce one new image to your environment and let it gently nudge your spirit every time you see it.
- Create a "dream box" filled with images that support your resilience and your dreams. Here's a little story about how I made mine and what happened as a result: When I was

in my mid-twenties, I took a beautiful robin's-egg-blue Tiffany box and made it into a "dream box." I decorated the outside of the box with symbols and images of things I hoped to attract into my life. Then I spent a few weeks filling the box with small visual representations of dreams I had, relationships I was longing to create, children I hoped to have, creative work I wanted to do, and even the house I hoped to have one day. For example, I put a little book I had made out of cardboard and one-inch pieces of paper into my dream box. I wrote the words MY BOOK on its little, itty-bitty cover. Countless times over the years, I took the dream box down from the top shelf in whatever closet I was living out of at the time and lovingly looked at and held all the little visual symbols. My dream box helped me to focus my thoughts and fueled my ability to visualize over time. I ended up living in a house that looks *exactly* like the Christmas ornament representative I put in my dream box, and I also have three children—two girls and one boy—to match the two miniature pink baby bottles and one blue one that I placed in the box. And you're holding in your hands the universe's response to that teeny-tiny book I made all those years ago. Using affirmations and visualization is like planting seeds—it can take time for the words and images you focus upon to germinate and take hold in the soil of the material world. But when you keep focusing thought-energy and loving feelings on what you've planted, you can be sure that your dreams will come to life. Make your own dream box today.

- Start your own collection of spiritually supportive books, images, and tools. Consciously growing your own spiritual library or "tool kit" is very empowering. Consider your collection an investment in your own bulletproof spirit.

● ● ●

Use Your Spiritual Radar

Follow your instincts. That's where true wisdom manifests itself.

—OPRAH WINFREY

SPIRITUALLY BULLETPROOF PEOPLE CULTIVATE AND RELY UPON THEIR own intuition for guidance in all areas of their lives. This "spiritual radar" helps them navigate life with more ease, grace, and effectiveness than their spiritually fragile counterparts. Less-resilient people tend to be unaware or dismissive of their own intuitive faculties and this limits their ability to respond to life's challenges. If you want to be as spiritually bulletproof as possible, it's essential that you begin to use and rely on your spiritual radar. You already possess all the "equipment" you need—you just need to figure out how to use it and learn to trust it.

If you don't feel connected to your own intuition, you are literally walking around handicapped. Intuition is not some "extra," "special," or "otherworldly" gift given to some people and not others—it is one of the basic senses you were born with to help you do your job as a human being here on Earth. There are people out there calling themselves "intuitives," but the truth is that we're *all* intuitives—we just don't all consciously claim and develop our intuitive faculties. Most people make the mistake of relying almost entirely on their rational minds for guidance. It doesn't take a genius to realize that this does them a serious disservice, although it *was* Albert Einstein who said that "The intuitive mind is a sacred gift and the rational mind is a faithful servant. We have created a society that honors the servant and has forgotten the gift." While they do value rational thought and logic, spiritually bulletproof people consciously, confidently, and consistently listen to and follow their intuition.

> Spiritually bulletproof people consciously, confidently, and consistently listen to and follow their intuition.

This doesn't mean that they discount input coming from other people or sources—resilient people are open to wisdom no matter how it arrives. But, in the end, they trust the voice of intuition more than any other.

A New Kind of Navigation

Making your way in this world is no easy task. There are so many decisions to make, relationships to negotiate, and choices to sift through. Especially when you've taken a hit, life can be a disorienting and difficult journey. Referring to the increasing complexity of the world around us, poet and cultural critic William Irwin Thompson writes that "More than ever, we need to have an internal sense of navigation." Trying to navigate the tempestuous sea of life without a well-developed intuitive faculty is like trying to circumnavigate the globe without a compass or a sextant; it is possible, but you certainly won't be making things easy for yourself.

When you journey through life without your intuition up and running at full speed, it's like trying to fly a plane across the Atlantic on a foggy evening without the benefit of radar. Intuition is a kind of spiritual radar. Think for a minute about what radar actually is and how it works. The word "radar" is an acronym derived from the words Radio Detection And Ranging and refers to the technique of using radio waves to detect the presence of objects in the atmosphere. These waves create an electromagnetic pulse that is focused and transmitted through the atmosphere. When that pulse "hits" something in its path, some of the energy is reflected back toward the radio waves, which then measure the returned signal. This allows us to "see" things that we can't see with our normal senses. The development of radar changed the world in a lot of profound and mundane ways—it allows us to travel safely by airplane and also lets us know if we need to bring an umbrella to work. You may not think a whole lot about the way radar makes your journey through life easier, safer, and more efficient, just like you may not think a whole lot about intuition and its influence on the quality of your life. But spiritually bulletproof people *do* understand the immense importance of their intuitive powers. They understand that their five senses are like compasses and sextants but that their intuition is like spiritual radar. It allows you to "see" much more fully than you can by relying on just your normal senses and rational thought. If you want to be able to respond with resilience to our fast-pace, rapid-change, super-complex world, then you need to figure out how to use your spiritual radar. And don't worry, you really do already have all the transmitters, receivers, and interpretive equipment you'll ever need—all you need to do is power them up and get comfortable using your inner technology.

Information Overload

Intuition is actually a pretty straightforward thing. It's really just about learning to listen to and completely trust your inner voice.

You'd think that something so simple would be fairly easy and commonplace, but that's not the case at all. Chances are, you are bombarded with so much information on a daily basis that your own intuition would have to scream bloody murder just to get your attention. Since intuition is not generally a screamer, preferring instead to whisper and hum, you can easily zip through days, months, and years of your life without ever consulting the best, brightest, and most brilliant part of who you are. And don't let the sheer volume and smarty-pants sound of all the information flying at you fool you into thinking that intuition is some second-rate way of evaluating what's going on. In fact, according to John Naisbitt, author of the international bestseller *Megatrends,* "Intuition becomes increasingly valuable in the new information society precisely because there is so much data." People in the know have known for millennia that intuition is the ultimate way of knowing, but intuition is anything but old-fashioned—it is a cutting-edge tool for people who want to cut through information overload. No one has more access to information in our world than Microsoft founder Bill Gates, and his philosophy is that "Often you have to rely on intuition." Now, more than ever, you need to be connected to your own intuition in order to navigate this accelerating, exhilarating, exhausting world. The irony is that it's harder than ever to establish and nurture that connection because of all the noise outside. It's an intuitive catch-22.

Solitary Refinement

American philosopher Hans Margolius writes that "Only in quiet waters do things mirror themselves undistorted. Only in a quiet mind is adequate perception of the world." Without solitude, it is almost impossible to cultivate a quiet mind. Your intuitive faculties will be stunted and stifled without solitude. Spiritually fragile people avoid being alone or they create a kind of mechanical isolation where they're lonely. They're unaware of the tremendous spiritual resilience that finds its foundation in solitude. Spiritually bulletproof people tap into the profound power of solitude and actively seek it out—they create time and space to be alone. They also understand that solitude must be an attitude in the midst of the crowd, not just a physical separation—they learn to listen to their inner voice even when they're surrounded by external chatter. Begin to view solitude as high-octane fuel for your resilience in general but especially for your intuitive powers.

The pace and tone of modern life can make trying to connect with your own intuition feel like trying to have a deep conversation about a sensitive topic with a fourteen-year-old while said teenager has earphones in his ears and is playing a video game on his PlayStation Portable. Italian poet and Nobel Prize winner Eugenio Montale points out that "Mass communication, radio, and especially television, have attempted, not without success, to annihilate every possibility of solitude and reflection." If you want to develop your own intuitive powers, you must begin by cutting out outside "noise." The most efficient way to do this is to create opportunities for solitude on a regular basis.

The School of Genius

The profound power of solitude has been recognized by many of the great minds and spirits throughout history. Ralph Waldo Emerson writes that "Conversation enriches the understanding; but solitude is the school of genius," and Laurence Sterne writes that "In solitude the mind gains strength and learns to lean upon itself." Begin to think about "alone time" as your chance to attend the School of Genius. Give your mind a chance to "lean against itself" rather than on the voices of other people. When you shut yourself off from the noise of the world and tune yourself in to the goings-on in your inner world, you open yourself up to a source of guidance and wisdom beyond all measure. There may be a lot of information coming at you from the outside, but the essential wisdom you need to navigate your life lies *inside.* Scottish scholar John Stuart Blackie writes that "Converse with men makes sharp the glittering wit, but God to man doth speak in solitude." Spirit really *will* speak to you when you get totally silent and ask for direction.

You can only benefit from this School of Genius if you actually attend classes. On a practical level, this means that you need to practice solitude regularly. Ideally, you will find time every day to be alone. Intuition thrives when you nurture it on a consistent basis. And though intuition does sometimes overwhelm us with its insistence and intensity, most of the time it nudges more than announces. Journalist and writing teacher Brenda Ueland believes that "inspiration does not come like a bolt, nor is it kinetic, energetic, striving, but it comes to us slowly and quietly and all the time, though we must regularly and every day give it a little chance to start flowing, prime it with a little solitude and idleness." If you're like most people, you're probably wondering how you're going to fit solitude and idleness into your schedule. But don't worry, a little goes a long way in these matters, and when your intuition is in prime shape, you will navigate life so much more easily and efficiently that you'll more than make up for the time you spend in solitude. In the School of Genius, an ounce of intuition is worth a pound of tuition.

Cosmic Fishing

Before you can catch a fish, you generally have to spend some time silently sitting on the water, waiting patiently for a fish to come to you. While you may actually reel in the fish very suddenly and quickly, what makes that moment possible is all of the quiet and passive moments that came before, as you let the waves gently rock your boat and kept your hook baited and ready. Fishing is a lot like tapping into your intuition. In fact, visionary Buckminster Fuller writes "I call intuition cosmic fishing. You feel a nibble, then you've got to hook the fish."

Spiritually bulletproof people learn to recognize the "nib-bles" of intuition so that they can "hook the fish." Spiritually fragile people are often so distracted that they don't feel the tiny tugs of their inner guidance and so they go home empty-handed. When you tap into your intuition, you are connecting with a source of knowledge and guidance beyond your own limited mind. Your rational thoughts are like the little boat that sits at the surface of the ocean that is your intuition. And don't make the mistake of dismissing this "intuition stuff" as New-Age nonsense—the greatest scientific minds have always acknowl-edged the power of intuition: According to Aristotle "Intuition is the source of scientific knowledge," and Albert Einstein writes that "The only real valuable thing is intuition." Dr. Jonas Salk, in-ventor of the polio vaccine, writes: "It is always with excitement that I wake up in the morning wondering what my intuition will toss up to me, like gifts from the sea. I work with it and rely on it. It's my partner." If you want to experience the full power of your bulletproof spirit, work with and rely on your intuition— make it your partner in all you do.

The Nuts and Bolts

The only thing standing between you and your intuition is a lack of *consciousness* and *confidence*. Consider these two critical differ-ences between people who identify themselves as highly intu-itive and people who do not:

1. Intuitive people *consciously* cultivate their intuitive faculties by spending time away from the noise of the crowd. They regularly seek out solitude and very often choose to spend time in nature, where they feel more attuned to their inner voice. Intuitive types frequently use meditation or some type of centering prayer to help them still their "monkey minds" and connect with the "still small voice" of spirit. They learn to recognize the subtle, gentle nudgings of in-

tuition and, over time and through practice, they develop a partnership with their inner guide.

2. Intuitive people have *confidence* in their own inner voice and have faith in its guidance. They pay serious attention to their own hunches, feelings, and "gut instincts," and rightly recognize them as intuition's way of communicating with them. They do not dismiss their own intuition just because rational thought or objective analysis doesn't necessarily support the message from their inner voice. They trust their intuition *implicitly.* They do not agonize over whether to trust the "little voice" that speaks to them when they go inward—they consider it a trusted partner and they do not hesitate to act upon its directives. Spiritually fragile people get the same messages from their intuition, but they either don't hear them or they lack confidence in their inner wisdom.

If you want to bounce back from the blow you've taken, your intuition knows how to get you there. If you've somehow lost connection with or confidence in your intuitive faculties, you can absolutely reclaim them and begin to reap the immense benefits that come when you partner with your intuition. When you learn to hear and rely upon your inner voice, you will be amazed at the ease and grace with which you will be able to navigate life and all of its challenges.

• • •

Bounce Back Boot Camp

Here are some ideas to help you get in touch with your own intuition:

- Spiritual teacher Florence Scovel Shinn believed that "Intuition is a spiritual faculty and does not explain, but simply points the way." Think of your intuition as a "You're getting warmer . . . okay, you're really getting hot now . . . yes, yes, you're burning up . . ." kind of guidance. Don't look for specific answers or expect information to come in complete and fully formed thoughts. One reason why so many people dismiss their own intuitive voice is that it often grunts rather than articulates. Many times, as Jonas Salk explains, "Intuition will tell the thinking mind where to look next." Start paying attention to even the faintest visceral reactions, and begin to acknowledge them when they "speak" to you. Honoring your intuition often means following "a whisper on the wind." It can sometimes feel like walking with a blindfold on. Try playing "Marco Polo" with your intuition, letting it redirect you when you start getting off course. You will learn to trust your intuition as you practice letting it lead you.

- Actor Kim Basinger has said that "I feel there are two people inside me—me and my intuition. If I go against her, she'll screw me every time, and if I follow her, we get along quite nicely." Using your journal, write a list of the times you can remember ignoring a "little voice" or not following a hunch. What happened as a result of you not honoring your intuition? Look over the list and forgive yourself for not listening to your inner voice. Now, try to think of a time in your life when you let your intuition overrule your intellect or other people's advice and things worked out for the best. Write about that experience and take a moment to thank your intuition for its wisdom and guidance. Tell yourself that you want more of these experiences.

- Take out your calendar or agenda and pencil in some solitude. Look over your week and actually schedule a period of solitude for yourself. It doesn't have to be long—one hour would be ideal but fifteen minutes is a start. When you actually take this solitude sabbatical, make sure that you really have an opportunity to get still enough that your inner voice might make an appearance. Get away from other people, make sure your cell phone is off, and be silent. This is not the time to window shop or distract yourself with external stimuli. If possible, get out into nature. Don't put any pressure on this time of solitude. Don't expect anything to "happen." Just let yourself "be" and enjoy your own company. Make a point of noticing how you feel when you're alone. Whether you get any messages or not, thank your intuition for always being with you, silently guiding you in all you do. Can you pencil in some solitude for yourself on a regular basis? Even five minutes of total silence every night before bed can make a profound difference in your ability to connect with your inner guidance.

- In the same way that sensory experiences—music for your sense of hearing, artwork for your sense of sight, gourmet cuisine for your palate—are a feast for your five senses, meditation is a feast for your sixth sense—your intuition. This is another great reason to begin or expand a meditation practice.

- There are some really great books to help you develop your intuitive faculties—anything by renowned intuitive Sonia Choquette is an excellent place to start. Her website, www.soniachoquette.com, has many practical resources to assist you. Laura Day is another tremendous resource—check out her website, www.practicalintuition.com, for books, products, and other tools to help you develop your intuition.

•   •   •

Respect Your Body—It's Your Ride Home

To keep the body in good health is a duty . . . otherwise,
we shall not be able to keep our minds strong and clear.

—BUDDHA

WE HOPE BY NOW THAT YOU SEE YOURSELF AS A BULLETPROOF spirit. When you identify more with your internal, spiritual self than you do with the external parts of yourself and your life, you connect with the truest security available to you. But just because you know that your true nature is spiritual doesn't mean that you disregard or disrespect your physical body. If you want to maintain a strong connection with your bulletproof spirit, you must also maintain a strong connection with your body. How you feel about, respond to, and treat your body has a profound impact upon your resilience and happiness. Your spirit and your body are inextricably linked—as Plato writes "We are bound to our bodies like an oyster is to its shell." If you want to reap the rewards of super spiritual resilience, you must begin to think of your body as your life partner and you must begin to treat that partner with love and respect.

Spiritually bulletproof people build strong partnerships with their bodies because they are clear about the true purpose of the body. This awareness shapes the way they think about and treat their bodies. Spiritually bulletproof people understand that the body's highest purpose is to serve as a vehicle for spiritual evolution.

> Spiritually bulletproof people understand that the body's highest purpose is to serve as a vehicle for spiritual evolution.

This does not mean that they don't enjoy their bodies. On the contrary, resilient people delight in the many experiences that the body makes possible. But spiritually bulletproof people are able to really love their bodies because they know that their bodies provide them with, above all else, the opportunity for spiritual growth. This view affects all of their beliefs about, attitudes toward, and choices regarding their bodies.

Body Blunders

As you begin to strengthen your bond with your body, you need to identify beliefs about or attitudes toward your body that undermine your resilience. Do any of the statements that follow sound familiar to you?

- My body is a source of dissatisfaction to me because I don't like what I see in the mirror.
- I push my body too much sometimes. I expect it to do what I want it to do even though I don't always give it the respect it deserves. I regularly deny my body proper nutrition and adequate rest.
- I say negative things to my body on a regular basis. I tell myself that I'm unattractive, fat, or disgusting.
- I am very preoccupied with what I wear. I don't like how I look in anything and I sometimes even avoid certain ac-

tivities, like swimming or exercising, because I don't like how I look in the clothing I would need to wear.

- I avoid sex because I am not comfortable with or confident about my body. I don't love my own body, so how can I believe anyone else will love it?
- I am afraid of getting older because I fear that my body will fall apart.
- I am frustrated with or angry at my body for not being healthy. I feel like it has betrayed me.
- I spend a lot of time thinking about how I look.
- I spend a lot of time "managing" the outside of my body. It's a lot of work to maintain the exterior.
- I crave touch. My body doesn't get enough attention or love.
- I wish I could just accept and love myself the way I am, but it's really hard.

If any of these statements resonate with you, you are not alone. Studies show that body dissatisfaction and body-image disorders are extremely common in our culture. The problem affects both men and women and even impacts growing numbers of young people. Check out some statistics that Central Michigan University cites in its training materials for residence life staff:

- *42% of elementary school students between first and third grades want to be thinner.*
- *80% of children who are ten years old are afraid of being fat.*
- *45% of women are on a diet every day.*
- *51% of nine- and ten-year-old girls feel better about themselves if they are on a diet.*
- *45% of men and 55% of women are dissatisfied with their physiques.*

As a society, we are rebelling against our own bodies! Many people have tense or adversarial relationships with their own bodies. Spiritually fragile people misunderstand the real purpose of their bodies and this creates discord. They may ignore their bodies' needs; burden their bodies with substances, activities, or behaviors that work against the body's true purpose; or focus only on the outer body and obsess over their appearance. For many different reasons, they do not create a healthy "marriage" between body and soul. If you're like most people, you've unconsciously internalized many unhealthy and warped messages about the body that do not serve you or your spiritual resilience. It's time to let go of these unhelpful and misguided notions so that you can make room for a new understanding that will help you to really love your body.

First Things First

Spiritually bulletproof people cherish and maintain their bodies because they believe that their bodies serve a sacred purpose. They agree with Thomas Edison's belief that "The chief function of the body is to carry the brain around," but they replace the word "brain" with the word "spirit." Like dance legend and choreographer Martha Graham, they believe that "The body is a sacred garment." Their motivation to care for their bodies is primarily spiritual and this makes a huge difference in their ability to stay motivated over time.

If you begin to think of your body as a temple for your spirit, many things begin to shift. When you start to appreciate the unbelievable miracle that your body actually is, it becomes unacceptable to treat it with anything less than reverence. If you're like most people, you do not see your body for what it truly is. Unless you can join Henry David Thoreau in saying "I stand in awe of my body," you do not really understand the great treasure that has been given to you by the universe. Getting to this realization is essential if you want to really connect with your bulletproof spirit and find the happiness you deserve. Oprah Winfrey says "I finally realized that being grateful to my body was key to giving more love to myself."

Being grateful to your body is the foundation of spiritual wellness. You cannot achieve spiritual health without having a healthy attitude toward your body. This does not mean that you need to have a fit body or an attractive body in order to have spiritual health—it means that you have to love and cherish your body no matter what its condition. When you love and cherish your body, you will naturally make choices and develop habits that make it likelier that your body *will* be more healthy, fit, and attractive, but a loving and accepting attitude is the foundation for all that comes after. Believe it or not, there are plenty of people who exercise and diet and look good, but who still do damage to their bodies by holding negative beliefs about themselves or by directing negative words at their own bodies. As long as you believe that the body is an adversary to be conquered or controlled, your spirit cannot help but be affected by living in such a stressful and negative environment. When you start to express your love and appreciation for your body, then your spirit will really begin to thrive and, miraculously, so will your body.

The Naked Truth

If you are like most people, you have spent years of your life trying to "manage" your body. You've probably approached your body "from the outside in" rather than from "the inside out," and this approach is guaranteed to leave you discontented with yourself and disconnected from your spirit. If you insist on being thinner or stronger or your skin clearing up before you are willing to really love yourself, you are setting yourself up for a lifetime of dissatisfaction. If you wait until you get all your external ducks in a row, you will never get around to the inner work that is what you're really here to do. Spiritually bulletproof people refuse to withhold love from themselves just because some part of their body isn't cooperating. Imagine withholding love or words of affection and approval from a child or a partner whenever they didn't live up to your highest standards—imagine the damage you would do to that relationship. The relationship you have with your body is the most intimate and important bond in your life—it deserves your unconditional love and respect.

Can you give your body unconditional love and respect? Gloria Steinem believes that "Each individual woman's body demands to be accepted on its own terms." Obviously, this is true for men, too. Can you accept your body on its own terms? This is very, very hard for most people to do and yet it is the basis for true self-esteem. As crazy as this may sound, a good place to start is by learning to love yourself naked. This doesn't mean that you look in the mirror and see physical perfection; it means that you see in your reflection a perfect vessel for your spirit. It also means that you make a mature and wise decision to respect your body because, stretch marks, saddlebags, and scars aside, it is the unbelievably complex and ingenious bio-chemical and electrical machine that allows your spirit to experience life, love, and the lessons you came here to learn. Stop for a minute right now and put your hand on your heart. Feel it beating and realize that it does this minute after minute, day after day, year after year, without any effort or direction on your part. How amazing is that? And it is this amazing machine that allows you the privilege and opportunity to continue to love and learn here on Earth. Even if you find it hard to say you *love* your body right now, maybe you can see that, at the very least, it deserves your *respect.*

It's totally normal to want to present yourself to other people in ways that make you look your best—I'm a big fan of candlelight, push-up bras, and sarongs at the beach. But if, in the privacy of your own bedroom or bathroom you cannot love and respect your body, you need to heal this wound. This doesn't mean that you need to give up on self-improvement—it's okay to want to look better and to make decisions and plans based on that desire. It's *good* to want to improve yourself *if*—and this is a big *if*—your desire to improve comes from a place of love and acceptance. Don't withhold love until you think you "deserve" it—

give yourself unconditional love and acceptance right now. You'll also be amazed at how much more successful your self-improvement efforts will be when you're already basking in the warmth of healthy self-approval. Learning to love yourself naked is not as crazy as it sounds. Carson Kressley hosts a show on Lifetime Television called *How to Look Good Naked,* which aims to help women accept and love their bodies. Even though the title is designed to be attention-getting, the show's real message is not so much about *looking* good naked as it is about *loving* yourself no matter what you look like naked. In our youth-oriented, "thin-is-in," beauty-obsessed society, you need to cultivate and channel your own inner Carson Kressley just to help you get through the day. The real way to look good naked is to see your body for what it really is—an amazing vehicle for your spirit's evolution. Start today to lovingly approve of yourself—naked and clothed—and give your spirit a happy house in which to dwell.

• • •

Bounce Back Boot Camp

Try these strategies for healing your perception of your body:

- Begin to treat your body as the temple that it really is. Johann Wolfgang von Goethe suggests that you "Take care of your body with steadfast fidelity. The soul must see through these eyes alone and if they are dim, the whole world is clouded." Let your choices regarding food, exercise, rest, and other body-oriented behavior be guided by an awareness of your body's real purpose. You will be amazed at how much easier it is to make healthy choices when your motivation is to give your spirit a healthy and happy home in which to live. Put a Post-it on your bathroom mirror and on your fridge that says: I LOVINGLY CARE FOR MY BODY BECAUSE IT IS THE HOME IN WHICH MY SPIRIT DWELLS.
- If you find that you have a negative attitude toward your

body, begin to give it love as a way of healing your misperception. For example, if you hate the extra fat around your midsection and look at yourself with disgust whenever you shower or get dressed, draw a heart or smiley face around your navel using a long-wearing lip liner or Magic Marker. No one will see it but you and it will remind you to stop directing rejecting and hateful energy at your own body. Whenever you see it, the heart or smiling face will remind you to pause and send some love and gratitude toward the stomach that enables you to digest the food you need to live. Use this technique with scars, stretch marks, or any other aspect of your body that you focus negative energy on. While the intent of this technique is to transform your perception, you will also be amazed to find that the love and acceptance you direct at your body may do more to transform it than anything else. It may sound goofy, but this exercise really works.

- Whenever you shower or bathe, get into the habit of thanking each part of your body as you wash it. From the hair on your head to the toes on your feet, spend a few moments giving some love and gratitude to each part of your miraculous body. If you find yourself being self-critical, use thought-stopping to redirect yourself—focus only on gratitude.

- Think about all of the things that your body gives you and makes possible that you take for granted. Do you even think about the fact that seeing and walking and breathing are things you probably just take for granted? As someone who deals with pain every day, I really appreciate the parts of my body that *do* work effortlessly and perfectly. Many people with serious illnesses or disabilities would do anything just to have their regular old, less-than-perfect but pain-free and healthy bodies back again. You don't need to experience loss of health or function to begin to appreciate your body—be vigilant about not taking your body for granted.

- Many people focus on diet, exercise, and grooming but forget to do the inner work of loving and respecting their bodies. Use the technique of visualization to support your body's wellness. Visualize yourself as healthy, fit, and strong. Use the power of your mind to assist your body in maintaining its vitality. If you need to lose weight to be healthier, do not focus on what you *don't* want to look like—picture yourself at the weight you want to be and keep that image in your mind. Put actual images of your ideal around the house to keep you motivated. Use positive and encouraging words to support your body as it transforms—put affirmations like I EASILY MAINTAIN MY IDEAL WEIGHT BY MAKING HEALTHFUL EATING CHOICES on your fridge.

- Think of exercise as "temple maintenance" and focus on the increased radiance it will give your spirit. Consider the attitude of my gorgeous and inspirational friend Gisela toward exercise. Since being diagnosed with both breast cancer and Parkinson's disease in the last five years—during which time she also suddenly lost her husband—Gisela has maintained her two-hour-a-day walking and yoga routine, though there absolutely were days when it would have been far easier to just lie on the couch. Though she has taken three of the most devastating hits imaginable, her radiance hasn't diminished in the least—in fact, her light is brighter than ever and it warms everyone she meets. Gisela does have a fit and lovely figure, but she gives herself the gift of exercise as a way of giving her body the love it deserves and caring for her spirit, too.

- If you're having a hard time loving or respecting your body, get Louise Hay's book *You Can Heal Your Life*. It has helped countless people to heal their perception of their bodies and better understand the relationship between their bodies and their spirits. Visit our website for links to Louise's website and many other helpful resources.

• • •

Act Like You Mean It

Do, or do not. There is no try.

—YODA

WELL, FRIEND, WE HAVE COME TO THE END OF THIS LEG OF THE journey together and soon you will put this book down. By now, we hope you know that you really *are* a bulletproof spirit and that you really *do* have all the inner resources you need to bounce back. There is one last secret that you need to know as you leave the pages of this book and go forward to live in a world where the bullets continue to fly and the hits keep on coming: Spiritually bulletproof people take action. They act upon what they know to be true and they realize, as Johann Wolfgang von Goethe did, that "Knowing is not enough; we must apply!" If you want the spiritual resiliency that can help you handle any hit that life hands out, you need to take daily action to apply the knowledge this book has given you.

There is a Native American proverb that says "A man must

make his own arrows." Once resilient people figure out what they're shooting for, they get to work making their own arrows. To bring their resilient thinking into real life, spiritually bulletproof people make it a habit to take daily action based on their knowledge and beliefs.

> Spiritually bulletproof people make it a habit to take daily action based on their knowledge and beliefs.

This doesn't mean that there aren't times when they want to stay on the couch or just curl up under a rock somewhere. Resilient people absolutely struggle with feelings of apathy and emotional paralysis just like everyone else—it's just that they take action even when they feel like doing nothing. Oliver Wendell Holmes touches upon this commitment to action when he writes "Greatness is not in where we stand, but in what direction we are moving. We must sail sometimes with the wind and sometimes against it—but sail we must and not drift, nor lie at anchor." Spiritually bulletproof people know, as Benjamin Disraeli did, that "Action may not always bring happiness, but there is no happiness without action."

Pray with Your Legs

If you want to find the happiness on the other side of the hit you've taken, begin today to take action on some of the knowledge you've gained by reading this book. You are much more aware now about the way that spiritually resilient people think and see the world, but it isn't enough to just be more aware—you actually need to transfer this awareness into action in your own life. And don't worry if some of the new ways of thinking about or doing things seem awkward or difficult at first—don't let that discourage you from sticking with them. Wise people have always understood that we learn by doing: Aristotle writes that "Excellence comes as a result of habit," and Ralph Waldo Emerson writes that "Skill to do comes of doing." The habits and be-haviors of spiritually bulletproof people will become easier and more natural for you if you just jump in and take them on.

Frederick Douglass was an American abolitionist, author, and reformer, as well as one of the most prominent figures in African American history. He was born a slave, escaped from slavery, and went on to devote his life to ending slavery in the United States. He knew that slavery was wrong and wanted to change his own plight and that of his fellow enslaved African Americans. He understood well the necessity for action in the face of adversity— he writes "I prayed for twenty years but received no answer until I prayed with my legs." If you want to free yourself from the suffering your hit has inflicted upon you, you also need to "pray with your legs." What we mean by this is that you need to become willing to take action in the face of your own fear, apathy, and depression. You need to be willing to *do* something—even if it's something small—every day to find your way through the hit you've taken to the happiness that is your destiny. As the poet Kahlil Gibran writes "A little knowledge that acts is worth infinitely more than much knowledge that is idle."

A Call to Action

Pulitzer Prize–winning author Annie Dillard writes that "How we spend our days is, of course, how we spend our lives." The only way to be spiritually bulletproof is, of course, to act like a resilient person on a daily basis. You don't need to worry about thinking and acting like a spiritually bulletproof person for the rest of your life—that is a very daunting proposition. You only need to think and act like a resilient person one day at a time.

Each of the secrets we've shared with you in this book is a call to action. The suggestions at the end of each chapter give you concrete and practical ways to apply the knowledge you've acquired. Some of the secrets will challenge you to push yourself to actions that may feel difficult or strange at first. Pay attention to the chapters that you struggled with most—very often, the thing you feel most resistant to is the very thing that might help you most. As Eleanor Roosevelt said "You must do the things you think you cannot do." For example, our experience has shown us how very critical forgiveness is to finding the happiness on the other side of whatever hits people have taken, and yet forgiveness is the very thing that most people resist. If you want to increase your spiritual resilience, you need to move things like forgiveness out of the realm of occasional thought and into the world of everyday action. Martin Luther King, Jr., believed that "Forgiveness is not an occasional act; it is a permanent attitude." The only way to cultivate a permanent attitude of forgiveness is to take action—to actually practice forgiveness on a daily basis. And this is true for all the secrets in this book—only by practicing the behaviors suggested will you really increase your resilience. Each chapter's Boot Camp section gives you concrete and practical ways to "do the things you think you cannot do," but only you can actually decide to *do* them. Ralph Waldo Emerson was right when he said that "No one can cheat you out of ultimate success but yourself."

Words to Live By

Each of the secrets in this book has a message that supports your bulletproof spirit. One easy way to take action every day is to simply reaffirm each of these messages. The words in these messages are powerful—they carry energy. Keep a list of these messages where you can reread it every day. Simply read the following list of affirmations *out loud* every morning or evening—in the two minutes it will take you, you will be sending a powerful signal inward to your spirit and outward into the universe. Pause between each message and take a deep, cleansing breath. Don't think about it—just take this simple action. Here's the list:

- *"I claim my birthright as an invincible spirit."*
- *"I am building myself a bulletproof mind."*
- *"I look for the gold hidden in every hit."*
- *"I build bridges from the hits I take to the happiness that awaits me."*
- *"The hits I take are an integral part of a purposeful life."*
- *"I recognize that my relationships are my greatest teachers."*
- *"I release feelings of entitlement that steal my energy."*
- *"I honor my grief by giving it the time and space it deserves."*
- *"My time in the fire is transforming and refining me."*
- *"I allow and honor all of my feelings."*
- *"I take charge of my space."*
- *"I let the sun set on my grief so that I can begin to live again."*
- *"I am ready to give myself the gift of forgiveness."*
- *"I realize with my real eyes so that I can forgive."*
- *"I see the best in people and catch them being good."*
- *"I deserve, seek out, and am given all the support I need."*
- *"I care for the needs of my soul by practicing good spiritual hygiene."*
- *"I embrace my desires while remaining detached from the outcome of my desires."*
- *"I get my Survivor Self, Sacred Self, and Synergizing Self together for regular chats."*
- *"I give myself the present of being present to the present."*
- *"I banish busyness to make room for the real business of living an authentic life."*
- *"I pay attention to and honor my attractions."*
- *"I am the hero of my life and I say yes to my adventure."*
- *"I nurture my spirit with a resilience-rich environment."*
- *"I listen to and follow my intuition at all times."*
- *"I love and respect my body because it's home to my spirit."*
- *"I act on my beliefs and knowledge."*

Simply reaffirming these messages every day will help you to connect with your bulletproof spirit. As you read the affirmations, notice which message draws your attention most and re-visit the chapter that deals with that message. Choose one exercise from the end of that chapter and make the time and space to actually do it. No matter how busy you are, give yourself the gift of taking action to support your bulletproof spirit—you're worth it. (Note: If you visit our website, you can download a printable version of these affirmations so that you can post them somewhere convenient.)

Invest in Yourself

Whether you are conscious of it or not, you are always investing in something. You have limited amounts of time, energy, and resources, and you are always in the process of investing them in one thing or another. The world is constantly sending you invitations to invest yourself in its myriad opportunities and, whether you realize it or not, you are constantly sorting through those invitations and making decisions about what deserves your attention and resources and what you will ignore. Think of the many things that you can invest not just money but also time and energy in: your home; your car, boat, or other "toys"; your career; your social life; your body; your hobbies; causes that you believe in—the list is really endless. St. Augustine writes in his *Confessions* about the concept of *multiplicity.* He warns of the dangers inherent in a multiplicity of good things—when there are so many essentially good things competing for our attention that we have no energy or time left for the very best things. This "multiplicity of goods" can actually make it difficult for you to invest in *yourself.*

There is nothing wrong with investing in your home, your career, your relationships, or your physical body. In fact, resilient people invest in all of these things and see them all as important elements of a good life. However, spiritually bulletproof people never get so caught up in the multiplicity of good things that they fail to invest in their own spiritual development. They actually make investing in themselves a priority, and this ensures that they keep their resilience high and remain able to handle whatever hits life hands out. You may feel guilty investing in yourself, or may wonder if it's selfish to make your own spiritual wellness a priority when there are so many other things that call for your time, energy, and resources. In reality, investing in yourself is really a wise and humble choice—it reveals a set of priorities that puts people before things, spirit before ego, and inner beauty before external appearances.

How do you invest in your own spiritual development? There are as many answers to that question as there are people to ask it, but a good place to start is by making *time* in your daily life to connect with your spirit. In our materially abundant culture, time is often the resource in shortest supply. Spiritually bulletproof people invest their precious *time* in their spiritual development. They read books, pray, and meditate; take time for reflection and solitude; attend services, workshops, and seminars; and take the time to figure out what their spirits need to keep growing. They also tend to invest some of their material resources in their spiritual development. When you spend money on electronics, CDs, clothing, cars, entertainment, furniture, and other material things, you are investing your money in assets that depreciate immediately upon purchase. But when you spend money on acquiring knowledge and experiences that increase your spiritual resilience, you are investing in an asset that appreciates year after year and that cannot lose its value. While they like nice things as much as anyone else, spiritually bulletproof people see the wisdom of making sure that they invest in their spiritual development, too. They have learned through experience that all things are vulnerable to the hits that life hands out, so they make it a priority to invest in the one thing that can never be taken from them—their bulletproof spirits. Begin today to invest in yourself—it will be the best investment you ever make.

The Path of Service

Our personal and professional experience has taught us that one of the most powerful ways to take action and come out on top of a hit is to explore the path of service. It is one of life's most miraculous ironies that we serve ourselves most of all when we reach out in service to others. And don't make the mistake of waiting until you feel completely recovered from your hit to start thinking about ways that you might be able to assist others; the path of service is also very often the path to healing ourselves. When Azim began working to prevent youth violence, his grief over his son's death was still raw and powerful but the work itself ended up being profoundly healing. I find that whenever I do a workshop or coach someone, I end up helping myself most of all through the experience. Don't worry if you aren't sure where to start and if you don't have a lot of energy at first. You don't need to run out and start a nonprofit. Just consider taking baby steps on the path of service. Maybe you can simply join a support group for others who've taken hits similar to your own— your presence to others going through pain is a kind of service that can make a profound difference in someone's life. Consider volunteering for a charity, nonprofit, or other organization whose work is connected to the hit you've taken; your personal experience may be a tremendous asset to such a group or organization. Think about starting a support group in your community for people who've taken hits in general—maybe you can organize weekly or monthly meetings where other spiritually bulletproof people can get together and support each other. If you feel too overwhelmed to take any outward action, the simple act of praying for other people in need is a beautiful way to serve others. Take a few minutes every day to send loving thoughts and healing energy toward someone you know needs it. You will find that, no matter how much or little you do in service to others, you will be made stronger and more whole for your efforts. You may also find that the path of service leads you to your life's purpose. Take the first step today.

Don't Forget to Play

One great way to take action is to make the effort and take the time to play. Play is powerful medicine—make sure you get your dose. As you begin to heal from your hit, it's really important that you remember to find ways to feel pleasure and joy. Especially after you've been dealing with adversity and pain, it is essential that you introduce some play into your life. At first, play may be the last thing on your mind and it may be hard for you to even think about doing anything fun. Many people going through adversity forget how to play and don't even know where to start. At first, you may have to act "as if" just to get yourself taking positive action. Act "as if" you want to actually engage in the play that you choose for yourself. In a way, it's like exercise—most people don't feel like exercising at first, but once they're doing it, they're glad they started. Make a point to schedule some activities that you generally enjoy, and you might even try out some new things that you're not sure about. Novelty can help arouse the pleasure centers in the brain. Go swimming—water is very healing and it's hard not to play a little when you're in the water. Do something you haven't done in years—maybe go bowling or ice skating. If you feel more sedentary, go to a funny movie or get a massage—the point is to do something that will get some feel-good chemicals going in your brain. When you've taken a hit, it can take a while for you to feel like playing, but you can really help yourself by giving yourself a nudge in that direction. Ask a friend to help keep you connected with the playful side of yourself—sometimes we need a nudge from the outside. Look at yourself as you would a beloved child and take action to give yourself the things that you know are healthy and helpful.

Ready for Action

Congratulations! By reading this book, you have demonstrated a serious commitment to your spirit and have already invested a lot of time and energy in trying to heal from the hit you've taken. The end of this book is really just the beginning of a journey you will take for the rest of your life as you put your new knowledge into action. We are so grateful to have shared this leg of the journey with you and look forward to being your partners on the road ahead.

This book is meant to be reread. You will get the most from this book if you use it as a regular part of your routine. Use the Boot Camp sections to help you develop new habits that will increase your resilience. Check out our website to keep yourself on course. Dealing with adversity is much easier when you have support and inspiration, and we hope you will find both when you visit us online. We want you to know that you are not alone; there are resources, both online and off, for inspiration and community. We hope you check out our website, share your story, offer support to others, or just browse through the many articles, downloads, and other resources on the site. We also provide links to many online resources that we hope will be of help to you in your spiritual development.

• • •

Bounce Back Boot Camp

Here are some ideas for taking action and investing in your spiritual development:

- When you plan your week or month, use your calendar to help you take action on your new spiritual knowledge. Actually pencil in time to do some of the activities or practices that we've suggested. Look through the Boot Camp sections in the book and choose five things you'd like to take action on. When you actually schedule time in your week or month to devote to your spiritual development, you are making an investment that will pay you amazing dividends.

- Become a part of a real-life group or online community of spiritually bulletproof people. Read this book with your book club, or if you don't belong to a book club, invite a few people to read the book and meet weekly to support each other as you get in touch with your bulletproof spirits. We have materials on our website for book clubs. Reach out and connect with other people. I've been in the same book club for the last seven years and know firsthand how these kinds of groups can support well-being.

- Take a baby step on the path of service. Reach out to help someone else in even a small way and see how much it will give you in return.

- If you've never taken a tele-class or attended a seminar or workshop on a spiritual topic, consider signing yourself up for one. Most spiritually bulletproof people consider themselves lifelong spiritual learners and make an effort to keep growing and developing. If you look around your community, you will find many opportunities to get involved locally. We have also put information and links on our website to help you find a wide variety of seminars and workshops around the country.

• • •

AFTERWORD

As you leave the pages of this book, we want to thank you for giving us the honor of your attention and for allowing us to share these experiences to you. We didn't write *The Secrets of the Bulletproof Spirit* only for the sake of writing a book—we also wanted to make a connection with our readers—*you*. The energies, emotions, and spirits of author and reader come together, here and now, when a book is received as it is intended, and we believe that it's important to acknowledge this exchange. As you continue your journey toward total connection with your bulletproof spirit, know that you are being lifted up and pulled along by the energy of many others who've come before, who've shared this book, and who are yet to come.

Namaste,   With Love,
Azim   Jillian

ABOUT THE AUTHORS

Following the murder of his son in 1995, AZIM KHAMISA founded the Tariq Khamisa Foundation and the subsequent forgiveness movement that has reached millions. In 2002 he received Search for Common Ground's prestigious Award for Building Better Communities. In 2004 he participated in the Synthesis Dialogues with His Holiness the Dalai Lama. And in 2006 came the Spirit of Crazy Horse Award from the Reclaiming Youth Network. Azim is also the recipient of the California Peace Prize. A sought-after speaker, he has spoken in person to more than a half million children. He lives in La Jolla, California.

As an Associate Minister at the Interfaith Temple in New York City, host of her own weekly radio talk show, and a life and spiritual coach, JILLIAN QUINN has touched the lives of thousands of people around the country with her workshops, classes, and coaching. She is a member of Spiritual Directors International and the recipient of a grant from the National Endowment for the Humanities for scholarship in the area of Transcendental Philosophy. She lives in Millbrook, New York, with her husband and three young children.